# REAL LIFE
# DINNERS

**ALSO BY RACHEL HOLLIS**
Upscale Downhome

# REAL LIFE
# DINNERS

*Rachel Hollis*

ST. MARTIN'S GRIFFIN
NEW YORK

www.stmartins.com

Photography: Kari Peters, Kate Noelle, and Jonathan Melendez
Design by Corey McClelland, with assistance by Sami Lane

THE LIBRARY OF CONGRESS CATALOGING-IN-PUBLICATION DATA IS AVAILABLE UPON REQUEST.

ISBN 978-1-250-15323-4 (trade paperback)
ISBN 978-1-250-15324-1 (ebook)

Our books may be purchased in bulk for promotional, educational, or business use. Please contact your local bookseller or the Macmillan Corporate and Premium Sales Department at 1-800-221-7945, extension 5442, or by email at MacmillanSpecialMarkets@macmillan.com.

First Edition: May 2018

10 9 8 7 6 5

For Daddy, who once made fajitas twenty-one nights in a row so he could "dial in" the recipe. Your commitment to flavor is just one of your many legacies.

# CONTENTS

# REAL LIFE DINNERS

# INTRODUCTION

My daughter is going to be born on Tuesday.

Today I'm sitting in a coffee shop feverishly trying to finish this cookbook, a second in my writing career, when I still can't believe I'm blessed enough to have gotten a contract for the first one. I say that I'm feverishly trying to finish, because my daughter is supposed to be born in six days and I've promised myself to be done before she arrives.

So many promises to keep.

I've promised a beautiful new cookbook to the fans who've been with me since the beginning. I've promised to meet my husband later tonight for a date, a special supper to commemorate the fifteen-year anniversary of our first date. I've promised my four-year-old that we'll play Candy Land on Friday after pizza. And I've promised my daughter's birth mother that I will be there to hold her hand while she labors to bring this baby I have prayed for for five years into the world.

The truth is that while figuring out the recipes and concept for this book was easy (because I can talk to you about food literally all day without once growing bored), dreaming up an opening chapter felt elusive. What more could I tell you about how much I love cooking, and how important I think it is for a family to cook and eat together, that I haven't told you already? I've grappled with it for weeks in between Googling "newborn adoption birth photography" approximately ten thousand times over the last two months. Between the writing of this book and the running of my company, there is karate practice, baseball and T-ball practice, and rehearsals for *West Side Story* (my oldest has four whole lines!). There's church on Sunday and date night on Thursday and our puppy still acts like the leash is a torture device rather than the key factor in our taking long strolls together some enchanted evening.

The majority of the time, it feels a little crazy, the idea that I'm spending every waking moment I can writing recipe intros and figuring out the right containers to hold a dish in the kid-friendly chapter, while also trying to keep up with my very real and hectic life. Sometimes I'm so busy working on ways to help *other women* live a better life that I run out of time and my kids eat turkey sandwiches—or worse, just straight-up turkey rolled around a piece of string cheese—for dinner. And in the midst of it all, we're (hopefully) adopting our daughter next week.

I say "hopefully" because we are at the end of four-plus years of trying to adopt. There were the two years we tried in Ethiopia before the country closed down its adoption program with the United States. There was the next year, when we mourned and tried to find another way. There was the year we spent getting certified to do foster-to-adopt in Los Angeles, where we live. There was the summer when we fostered two sisters and then managed the grief when they transitioned back. Then there was the early fall when we were placed with newborn twin girls we thought would be ours forever—truly one of the happiest experiences of my whole life. And then came the time *after*, when they, too, left because of a reconciliation with their birth family. I know that God has a plan for their lives and this was always meant to be it . . . but I mourned the loss as if someone had died.

Now I find myself here, in this small coffee shop, trying to finish this book so I can fly to Nebraska to be with the birth mom who has chosen us to be her baby's parents. Hopefully.

Hopefully, because this could all change in a moment.

No part of adoption is ever easy or guaranteed.

She could change her mind.

I say this to myself at least fifty times a day.

I remind myself to use caution, to temper my enthusiasm in case it doesn't work out like I hope it will. I have a long history of reminders that life isn't often kind or even fair. Not fair to a family like ours with so many failed adoptions. Not fair to the mamas who must make the brave but brutal decision to give up their babies in the first place. Life is often hard and rarely is it fair.

But what does any of this have to do with a cookbook full of dinner recipes?

Because real life isn't a series of stylized air-brushed photos. Real life is crazy, chaotic, hard, beautiful, funny, weird, shocking, devastating, and it can knock you right off balance.

But for me, cooking and eating as a family (even those turkey sandwiches) has always brought me back to center.

My dinner table is a touchstone.

My dinner table is *the cornerstone* of my life.

No matter how crazy my life gets, a good dinner makes me feel like we're going to be okay. Making sure my family is fed is a success, but truly taking the time to give them something wholesome and delicious is me at my best.

Not delicious and served on china. Not wholesome and produced by a mom with full makeup and hair. Not dinner made in a clean kitchen. Just made, with love and care, by me . . . that's the bar I set for myself. I don't get there every day—not even close—but it's my pursuit . . . to cook and eat great food with my family and friends, and any day I get there feels like a day where I'm winning.

In my real life, both my husband and I work and we have three people to feed other than ourselves. Real life means creating dinner can't take hours. Real life means there's no way I can marinate or prep a day in advance unless it's a special occasion. Real life means nothing is from a starter. Real life means I want to know what is actually in the food I'm eating . . . . It may not be low calorie or organic, but I want to use wholesome ingredients. Real life means the dish needs to work for all of us.

So I'm sitting here in this coffee shop trying to figure out this opening chapter, and I thought, *Well, what would you want to tell your daughter about these recipes?* My hopeful heart skips a beat at the idea that I might have the chance.

What I'd tell her is that the moments when you sit down and find your center will always bring you back to yourself. No matter how hard life gets or where it takes you, you need a place you can come back to and feel like yourself.

For me, that's food . . . or more specifically, that's *dinner.*

Years ago, on our second trip to Florence, a local told us about a restaurant in her neighborhood. After wandering cobblestone streets and asking for directions in painfully bad Italian, we found this darling little place I still can't recall the name of. We were ushered inside out of the cold and bundled into a bustling and joyfully crowded family-owned place.

What followed was a four-hour meal with more decadent courses than our stomachs could hold and wine that flowed like the Nile.

The evening when I brought my first son home from the hospital, I ate an entire pot of chicken and dumplings—by myself. My mother made the dish for me for dinner every single time I brought a baby home from the hospital.

As a little girl, I would spend long weekends with my grandparents. To this day, there isn't a better comfort food than my Grandma Neeley's ham sandwich on white bread with cream of chicken soup on the side. I've tried to make it for myself in the years since she went to heaven, but it's just not the same without her.

Once, my mom took the boring frozen chicken patties she got on special at Costco and deep-fried them in Crisco. She served those golden, delicious masterpieces with mashed potatoes and gravy. I'd get a forkful of gravy and potatoes and then stab a piece of chicken, making a sort of delicious top hat of food. It still makes me hungry to think about that bite, twenty-eight years later.

My big brother Ryan was the one who taught me to put a slice of American cheese on my potpie to make it extra tasty. "It'll melt down into a little cheese blanket," he told me. "The blanket will be your favorite part." He was so, so right.

After I ran my first marathon, we ate homemade tacos and a triple-layer cake I had them ice with "26.2."

After our wedding, Dave and I snuck back to our hotel room and ordered a club sandwich with fries and ranch dressing. There's never been a better sandwich in the history of time or space than the one we ate huddled in our wedding clothes that night.

After weeks of traveling around Europe on vacation with friends, I found a McDonald's in Nice, and homesickness made the hamburger one of the best burgers I've ever had.

So many stories . . . hundreds that I can recall, and others are buried deeper down. They get unearthed through a particular smell or the use of my grandpa's favorite platter.

What do these memories have in common? They're some of my favorite meals.

They're also—every single one—something I ate for dinner.

I have so many incredible memories wrapped up in food—but the memories of my favorite dinners are long enough to go on for hours. In fact, if we're ever enjoying a happy hour together or making small talk at a party, you can bet that I'll ask you to tell me about your favorite dinner.

There's just something so special about supper. Typically we work harder to create dinner. We tend to put more effort into its construction and sometimes spend whole days dreaming up exactly what it will be. Friendships flourish around dinner. Relationships start because of it.

It is, hands down, one of my favorite things in this life.

Not my favorite meal, or my favorite way to use a recipe . . . literally, my favorite thing. Period.

When I was a little girl, we sat down to a dinner cooked by my mama every single night of the week. We ate things like pot roast or baked chicken when we had the money. We had recipes like pinto beans and fried potatoes when we didn't. The simple dishes were served up with a side of sliced white bread or tomatoes fresh from the backyard. The things on our dinner table were never, ever fancy. But the meal itself was a big deal. We came together every evening as a family, we absorbed table manners, we learned how to make conversation and how to behave with as much maturity as we could squeeze into our tiny immature bodies. Thirty years later, even with the pain of my parents' divorce and the loss of my big brother, we can still come together for dinner; can still fall into the familiar, comforting routine of sharing a meal, because it's the foundation of who we are as a family.

The dinner table is sacred.

I didn't understand that as a child, but I fully recognize it now as an adult. There is something incredibly special—holy even—about gathering together to share a meal in your home. No matter your age, your relationship status, or the cost of the dinner you're serving, it's an opportunity to be together and connect. It's why I wanted to devote an entire cookbook to dinner. Well, that, and the fact that it's one of the biggest questions in my house on the daily. *What's for dinner?* Everyone wants to know. Sometimes we haven't even had lunch yet and already we're trying to figure out our dinner. Dinner cookbooks are the only kind I tend to buy. Dinner recipes are what I look up on Pinterest. It's the area I want to master and constantly add to. If dinner isn't a big deal to you one way or the other, you may question why anyone would care this much. But for those of us who do care, mastering family dinner is a *big deal.*

Being a wife, partner, or mother is so daunting at times. I remember spending the early days of my marriage trying to cook food I'd never had before but that my husband, Dave, loved.

I destroyed the fillets. I burned the pork chops to a crisp. We ate undercooked rice and overcooked pasta more nights than I can count. And every single time I didn't get it right, every single time it came out so wrong, I felt terrible. I come from a long line of great cooks . . . so how come I couldn't accomplish this one simple task? Feeding the people I love feels ingrained in my DNA; it feels like something I

*shouldn't* struggle with. But those early days of finding my way in the kitchen . . . I struggled so much! I've cried harder over a ruined turkey than I ever did watching *The Notebook*.

So this place I find myself now, where I feel confident in what and how I feed my family, feels like an accomplishment. Understanding what brings me joy, and also what can bring me solace, is hard won as well. What I'd hope for my daughter, and my sons, and anyone who might be reading is that you would feel confident in your own kitchen and you'd use your skills to build community around a table.

It doesn't begin with elaborate dishes that take eight days to prep. It begins with simple food, wholesome ingredients, and a desire to enjoy a meal with people you care about. This is relevant in times of celebration and essential even in times of mourning. What I'd tell my daughter is that I wrote this cookbook for women like me who care quite a bit about what's on their plate but have real-life scenarios that inhibit how much time they can spend to get it there.

I'd tell my daughter that there are recipes in here that we can use when we're celebrating and happy. I'd tell her that there are also favorites from my childhood that have always been my fallbacks when life was more difficult. I'd tell her that regardless of what happens next Tuesday, the foundations of my family—built around our old kitchen table—will remain strong.

As I write these words, I'm hopeful that the remainder of this book will be filled with pictures of our family, finally complete after so many years of praying for a daughter. I'm imagining me prepping dinner with a little baby girl with dark hair strapped to my chest. I'm praying that the recipes I grew up loving and have grown into making will be as important for her as they are for her brothers. I don't know what will happen next week but I know that this family—our traditions, and our recipes—will live on through stories and pictures and flavors that stretch back for generations before she or I were ever born.

# TABLE MANNERS

I'm just going to say it: I'm silently shocked at how bad many people's table manners are. I'm not talking about, like, Vikings. I'm talking about everyday humans that I sit down with at business dinners or friends of mine that I'm too afraid to correct for fear of embarrassing them.

For years I've thought about saying something . . . maybe with a post on the site or a helpful video, but then I worry that people will think I'm a snob or that I'm judging them. But . . . if I had something stuck in my teeth, I'd want you to tell me that there was something stuck in my teeth. Also, my daddy always said that you could pretend to be something all day long, but the second you held your fork the wrong way, people would know how uncouth you actually were. We might have been from out in the sticks, but he was insistent that we behave at the table from the moment we were old enough to sit there alongside him.

As a child, I thought he was a bit of an ogre when it came to barking at us about the right way to hold our knife when we were cutting a piece of meat. As an adult, I get it.

Table manners matter.

It's something we have instilled in our boys from the time they were little. They say "Yes, ma'am" and "No, sir," and they know to keep their elbows off the table, the napkin in their lap, and how to cut their meat. Maybe, like my boys, you know all of these details already, but if you don't, then I want to share some basic tips for great behavior at the table. This is a must (yes, *a must,* blame my Southern roots) for anyone raising children and a great reminder to polish up even if you're a grown-up.

So here are some basic table manners, which aren't written out as Emily Post would, but are definitely written exactly as I'd teach them to my kids.

1. Don't talk with your mouth full . . . or even partially full. Shoving your bite into the corner of your cheek like an able-bodied squirrel doesn't clear it of food enough for you to speak. I know your story is exciting, but swallow before you continue to tell us about the *Minecraft* world you built today.

2. Don't reach across anyone else's plate. I know you see the mashed potatoes. I know your arms are long enough to grab it yourself. Resist the urge. Simply ask the person whose plate is between you and your heart's desire to please pass the item over.

3. If someone asks you to pass them something (the ketchup, the rolls, etc.) you *may not* help yourself to it before handing it over. Even if their asking makes you think, *Well, yes, sauerkraut would be a lovely addition to my plate, too, and since it's here in my hands I might as well put it to use.* No. Hand it to them first and then politely ask for it back when they're finished.

4. For the love of all that is holy, keep your elbows off the table! If dinner is over and you're all hanging out, feel free to get more casual. But as long as we're having a meal you better keep your knobs out of plain sight. This is the dinner table, not the corral fence . . . . Keep your arms in the proper position.

5. Your napkin goes in your lap . . . yes, even if it's paper. Yes, a napkin is required. Always.

6. The old idea that you should wait until everyone has been served isn't actually true. You should wait until *three people* at the table have their plates, then you should begin eating. There is nothing your host or hostess would hate more

than for all of your food to get cold while you wait on everyone else. It's sort of like pickup basketball . . . once you've got a few people, you're ready to go.

7. Don't be gross. In our house we have a hot-sauce rule . . . if you do or say gross things at the table you get a dab of hot sauce on your tongue. "Gross" includes things like: the release of any bodily gas or fluid, talking about the release of any bodily gas or fluid, telling stories that make it hard for the rest of us not to gag, and so on. To this date, not one of my children has ever had hot sauce . . . not because they haven't done a hot sauce–worthy offense . . . but because it's more the threat of hot sauce, or the urban legend of hot sauce, that keeps their manners (at least mostly) in check.

8. Bring your food to your mouth, not your mouth to the food. The food on your fork isn't your great white whale, it's not something you have to chase after. It should come to you.

9. Use your indoor voice. Just like in kindergarten, there are inside voices and outside voices . . . the table is a place for inside voices. I'm all for lively conversations and getting excited, but when my kids start to yell over the top of each other it goes from an enjoyable experience to something stressful. So, I encourage conversation, but I ask that they keep it within the appropriate decibel range.

10. Wait your turn to speak. The reason I insist on instilling table manners in my children is because I'm trying to raise them to be functioning members of society. I shudder to think of them being invited to a friend's house for dinner and hollering over the top of someone else. This is something you can practice, even with toddlers, to teach them how to make conversation in a polite way.

11. No technology at the table. Come on guys, I know it's hard, but you shouldn't bring anything with an on/off switch to the table. It's so rude. It's so distracting. It pulls you out of the moment with your family (when you probably get too few already) and pulls you onto Facebook. So, our house rule is no tech at the table. We use the time (at least try) to actually converse with each other.

12. Conversation is a must. Conversation is the *whole* point of having dinner together! Ever since our kids were little we've encouraged this by asking them about their favorite and least favorite part of the day. Giving them this opener means even little people can join in. It's also a great way for us to learn about something that might be bothering them or for them to learn how we as adults manage a difficult task or the things we're excited about.

13. Whoever cooks does not clean. While not necessarily table manners, this is a polite gesture my children need to learn now. If you didn't help get dinner on the table, then you're on cleanup duty. The boys work as a team doing age-appropriate chores to get the kitchen back in shape. My oldest will load the dishwasher while the middle clears plates and glasses and the four-year-old puts (nonbreakable) items on the counter that Daddy helps to put away. This same rule applies when we go to other people's houses for dinner. The offer to help clean up is ingrained in their behavior because they have to do it at home.

14. Lastly—but most importantly—say thank you! If someone made you dinner or bought you dinner or just fixed you a sandwich, for heaven's sake, say thank you.

# KITCHEN ESSENTIALS

In my first cookbook, I devoted a whole chapter to hostess essentials. I listed everything I could think of that a host or hostess might need to entertain at home—from platters and plates to napkins and fancy straws. Since this book is devoted to dinner, I would be remiss if I didn't also include a list of items you can keep in your pantry, freezer, or fridge for extended periods of time that can easily add flavor, texture, or nutrients to your recipes. Just like with the list in my last cookbook, I'm not suggesting that you run out and buy all of these items tomorrow. Instead, keep an eye out for when these go on sale and build a stockpile then.

## IN THE PANTRY

1. Dried Pasta — In an absolute pinch, I can make dinner for my kids with pasta, butter, and some Parmesan cheese. The rest of the time my pasta is on hand for spaghetti, mac 'n' cheese, and even as the addition to a soup to make it heartier.

2. Olive Oil, Coconut Spray, and Ghee — Say what? What on earth is "ghee"? And why coconut spray? What's wrong with good ole nonstick cooking spray? In the last year I've become so much more mindful of what's in my food. For instance, the nonstick cooking spray I've used my whole life has silicone in it. As in, I'm spraying silicone in a pan and then mixing my food around in it. The vegetable or canola oil I always reached for when sautéing? You don't even want to know the chemical process it has to go through to be that clear golden color. So I've started using these three items—olive oil, coconut spray, and ghee (clarified butter)—to cook with, and we made the change with minimal fuss.

My only exception to this rule is that I still fry my chicken in Crisco because it's a family recipe, but since it's only every once in a while, I consider it a million times better than the cooking products I was using before.

3. Spices and Herbs and Seasoning, Oh My! — Flavor is everything, you guys . . . everything. Seasoning can take a basic protein to new heights. It can turn a basic olive oil into a dip for some crusty bread. It can garnish your cocktail rim and give you the fortification you need to eat your veggies. Make sure you have the basics: garlic powder, onion powder, dried basil, dried thyme, chili powder, chili pepper flakes, kosher salt, and peppercorns for fresh ground pepper. Look for bottles that don't have anything extra (like sugars or chemicals) and experiment with your dishes every time you cook to find out which combinations you like most.

4. Canned Goods — Tomatoes, Ortega chiles, corn, black beans, tuna, or anything else you like to mix with rice, stews, soups, salads, and pastas. Canned products are awesome to keep on hand because it's an easy way to liven up almost any dish you're cooking. Last year I gave up eating meat as a test, and almost immediately I felt so much better. The only kicker is that everyone in my family still eats it, and sometimes I just don't have the energy to prep two separate meals for us. I'll make dinner and then pull out some canned beans or tuna to add to our veggies and rice as my dinner while they're all enjoying the steak.

5. Vinegar — There are so many to choose from: balsamic, apple cider, white wine, red wine; and they all come in handy. Balsamic is essential in my favorite pot roast and crispy Brussels sprouts recipe. Apple cider has approximately four thousand at-home uses, and white and red wine are both great in salsas and sauces.

6. Canned Broth — Stock up on chicken, beef, or vegetable broth, depending on

what you're into. Broth is a key ingredient in so many recipes or a quick base for a soup, so it's worth keeping some on hand.

7.  Things That Crunch — Sunflower seeds, slivered almonds, chopped pecans, etc., are all great healthy additions to salads. There's something about the crunch of them that sort of tricks my brain into believing I'm having tortilla chips or croutons, so I always keep them handy in my pantry.

8.  Easy Healthy Add-Ins — I'm a big fan of nutrients I can hide in my food, which is why I always have bags of chia seeds, ground hemp, or flaxseed on hand. I mix them into anything I can to add fiber, antioxidants, or other nutrients to whatever I'm eating.

**IN THE FRIDGE . . .**

1.  Jars of Peppers — Tamed jalapeños, sliced pepperoncini, and roasted red peppers are always in my fridge. The tang of any of these can add pizazz to my meal or some much-needed color to a bland dish without adding a bunch of extra calories or fat.

2.  Pickles — Dill, sweet, spears, relish, you name it: it's currently hanging out in the door of my fridge. These work much like the peppers but with a milder flavor my kids can enjoy.

3.  Chopped Garlic — Don't get me wrong, I love fresh garlic as much as the next gal. But sometimes I don't have that kind of time (nor do I want my fingertips to smell like an osteria for the next three days), so I keep a jar of chopped garlic on hand.

4.  Mustards — Whole grain, Dijon, yellow, spicy . . . my mustard list is almost as

long as my pickle lineup. I'm forever looking for flavor without fat, and mustard wins every time.

5. Hard-boiled Eggs — Technically, these aren't as long lasting as the other items on my list, but they're a staple in my fridge, so it feels like a good item to include here. I can turn my hard-boiled eggs into deviled eggs or egg salad. I can chop them up and add them to tuna or mixed greens. In a pinch, I can eat one on the plane as a snack or for some protein, so every Sunday when I prep for my week, I always make five or six HBEs to have on hand.

# RACH'S SPICES

I'm a tiny bit obsessed with spice blends, you guys. Spice blends take a lot of the guesswork out of adding flavor to your dish and can boost the most basic protein from boring to bomb! Now, you can absolutely buy spice blends premixed from the store but if you're into it (and if you've already got individual spices taking up room in your cupboard) consider mixing up your own batch. All of the spice blends I reference in the book are my own creation—feel free to use store-bought or use a recipe below to make your own. Extra credit if you make a big batch and then give them away as gifts. . . In that instance you can fully tell people that they're your own creation. I don't mind at all.

From Left: Moroccan Blend, Zesty Italian, Southwestern Ranch, Fiesta Blend

# FIESTA BLEND

*Makes: ¼ cup*

*2 tablespoons nutritional yeast (available in health food stores, and optional, but it makes it taste great)*

*1 tablespoon dried lemon zest*

*1 tablespoon dried parsley*

*1 tablespoon dried red bell pepper*

*2 teaspoons garlic powder*

*1 teaspoon onion powder*

*1 teaspoon dried minced onion*

*1 teaspoon ground cumin*

Mix all the ingredients together and store in an airtight container in a cool dark place.

# SOUTHWESTERN RANCH

*Makes: ¼ cup*

*1 tablespoon onion powder*

*2 teaspoons ground chipotle powder*

*2 teaspoons dried lemon zest*

*1 teaspoon garlic powder*

*1 teaspoon dried chives*

*1 teaspoon dried minced onion*

*1 teaspoon dried parsley*

*1 teaspoon ground black pepper*

*1 teaspoon ground cumin*

*¼ teaspoon dried dill*

Mix all the ingredients together and store in an airtight container in a cool dark place.

# ZESTY ITALIAN

*Makes: ⅓ cup*

*1 tablespoon dried basil*

*1 tablespoon garlic powder*

*1 tablespoon dried minced onion*

*1 tablespoon onion powder*

*1 teaspoon ground black pepper*

*2 teaspoons dried oregano*

*1 teaspoon dried lemon zest*

Mix all the ingredients together and store in an airtight container in a cool dark place.

# MOROCCAN SEASONING

*Makes: ⅓ cup*

*1 tablespoon dried parsley*

*1 tablespoon ground coriander*

*1 tablespoon dried garlic powder*

*2 teaspoons ground turmeric*

*2 teaspoons chili flakes*

*1 teaspoon ground black pepper*

*1 teaspoon ground cumin*

*1 teaspoon ground paprika*

*¼ teaspoon ground nutmeg*

*¼ teaspoon ground allspice*

*¼ teaspoon ground cinnamon*

Mix all the ingredients together and store in an airtight container in a cool dark place.

# BREAKFAST FOR DINNER

I must have been seven or eight years old—I can't be sure of my exact age, only the awareness that I was small enough that the milkshake felt almost illicit.

We'd been on a family road trip for what felt like weeks, but that's got to be a child's recollection . . . no way my parents would suffer being trapped with four kids for that long. It was likely just a matter of days. At the end of a long day of traveling in our blue minivan, we pulled into the parking lot of a diner. This was incredible because we never, ever went out to a real restaurant. With four kids and a tight budget, dinner outside of our own kitchen was a rarity. This particular night is the first time I can remember eating at a restaurant in my whole life. I'm not saying it didn't happen very rarely. When a grandparent turned a new decade, I'm sure we went to the Olive Garden or something, but this particular night is my first restaurant memory. Even more startling, my mother told me I could order anything off the menu.

*Anything*, you guys.

We didn't have the money for anything . . . even at Denny's. We had the money for a kid's plate you split with your sibling and water from the tap. Also, I didn't have *anything* kind of parents. I had you'll-eat-it-and-you'll-like-it kind of parents. This experience was unprecedented. The power felt awesome.

How would I ever choose? *What* would I ever choose?

I chose a chocolate milkshake and French fries . . . for dinner. And she let me! My mother let me order that for dinner without batting an eyelash. Maybe she was feeling the magic of vacation. Maybe she was exhausted from trying to manage all of us kids and she'd just given up. Or maybe she was tippling from a flask in the glove compartment, who knows? All I know for sure is that the memory of having something for dinner that wasn't really dinner felt special . . . felt so significant that I remember it twenty-eight years later. Pizza at three o'clock in the morning, or cake for breakfast (because, let's be honest, that's what doughnuts are!) or your favorite egg dish at suppertime. It feels special. It's also, at least for me, way easier to make breakfast than some elaborate dinner feast. We have "brinner" (that's breakfast for dinner, yo) at least once a week. Not so much the milkshake. It might bring all the boys to the yard, but it's yet to show up on our dining room table disguised as a meal.

# B.L.A.T.E.

Bacon? Yes. Lettuce? Okay, fine. Avocado? By the truckload! Tomato? To-mah-to! Egg? You went and added an egg? And then let it drip down the side of your sandwich like that scene in *Spanglish* where Adam Sandler makes a sandwich in the middle of the night that I'm still hungry for a decade later? Yes. Yes, I did! Y'all, I can't imagine you need me to convince you of the magic of this sandwich, but perhaps you just need me to remind you that a BLT is a great and easy option for dinner, and if you have the avocado or eggs handy, it's only going to add to the overall experience.

# INGREDIENTS

8 slices whole-grain sandwich bread

olive oil, optional

½ cup prepared pesto

¼ cup mayonnaise

4 small tomatoes (thinly sliced)

12 strips thick-cut bacon (cooked until crispy)

1 ripe avocado (sliced)

4 leaves green-leaf lettuce (washed and dried)

4 eggs (cooked over-easy)

# DIRECTIONS

1. Toast the bread in a toaster, or heat a skillet over medium heat with a touch of olive oil. Toast each piece of bread in the skillet until golden brown on one side.

2. For each sandwich, spread 1 slice with pesto, and the other slice with mayonnaise.

3. Next, layer each sandwich with bacon, tomato, lettuce, avocado slices, and top each one with an over-easy egg.

4. Finally, top each sandwich with the second slice of bread, and serve immediately.

 **15** MIN *Prep Time*

 **15** MIN *Cook Time*

 **4** SERVINGS *Makes*

# PESTO INGREDIENTS

⅓ cup olive oil

½ teaspoon salt

¼ teaspoon pepper

¼ cup pine nuts

1 clove garlic (minced)

¼ cup grated Parmesan cheese

2 cups basil leaves (4 ounces)

# PESTO DIRECTIONS

5. Place all the ingredients listed into a blender or food processor in the order listed.

6. Blend on low or pulse until the pesto comes together, but is still a little chunky.

7. Transfer the pesto to an airtight container. Refrigerate and use within 3 days.

# BREAKFAST PIZZA

This idea came to me years ago upon remembering a breakfast pizza from Schwans. Did you guys ever order anything from Schwans? In my hometown you were super fancy if you got a delivery from those guys . . . and my family was never going to be fancy, okay? I idolized that truck of frozen delicacies, one of which was a mini breakfast pizza. We remade it years later with our cool spin (shout-out to the cast-iron skillet!) and I'm happy to report that it's delicious enough that you could serve it to guests for dinner and they'd be ecstatic to receive Tater Tots on a pizza.

# INGREDIENTS

1 pound store-bought pizza dough

1 cup Tater Tots, fried or baked

4 slices thick applewood-smoked bacon, cooked and cut into small pieces

3 slices Canadian bacon, cut into small pieces

2 tablespoons olive oil

5 slices provolone cheese

3 large eggs

salt and black pepper, to taste

fresh chives, snipped, as garnish

fresh thyme leaves, minced, as garnish

# DIRECTIONS

1. *Preheat oven to 450°F. If you have a pizza stone, place it in the oven to preheat, as well. Take pizza dough out of the fridge and let it sit at room temperature for 30 minutes.*

2. *Meanwhile, prepare remaining ingredients. Cook Tater Tots and applewood-smoked bacon. Slice Canadian bacon. Set aside until dough is ready.*

3. *Place 1½ tablespoons olive oil into 12-inch cast-iron skillet. Place room-temperature pizza dough inside skillet. Pat into a disk using the palm of your hand.*

4. *Stretch dough out, starting from the center, rotating dough in the skillet to form an even 12-inch circle. If the dough is still too elastic, cover lightly with plastic wrap and let dough rest for 5 to 10 minutes.*

5. *Use remaining ½ tablespoon of olive oil to coat the top of pizza dough.*

*Place provolone cheese slices on top, followed by sliced Canadian bacon and applewood-smoked bacon. Arrange Tater Tots in such a way to allow room for cracked eggs.*

6. *Place skillet over the stove on medium heat, and cook for about 4 minutes. Prop the pizza up every other minute or so to check on the underside of the dough. After 4 minutes, the bottom of the pizza should be set and lightly golden brown in color. The oil should always be bubbling as this point.*

7. *Remove the skillet from the stove. Crack eggs onto the pizza. Season pizza with salt and black pepper. Place in oven for 8 to 10 minutes until the cheese is bubbling and melted, and the egg whites are cooked through. Let cool slightly in skillet before transferring to cutting board to cut into slices. Garnish with thinly snipped chives and chopped thyme.*

 *Prep Time*

 *Cook Time*

 *Makes*

# BREAKFAST QUESADILLAS

I really appreciate quesadillas because I always have cheese and tortillas in my fridge. I really appreciate *breakfast quesadillas* because they're an easy way to add protein and excitement to a basic dish. In this instance we used chorizo, which adds incredible heat and depth of flavor, but you can feel free to swap it out for bacon, ham, or go meat-free!

# INGREDIENTS

½ pound chorizo

1 cup diced red bell pepper

1 cup diced zucchini

2 cups sliced mushrooms

½ cup corn, frozen or canned

½ cup sliced scallions

6 eggs

¼ teaspoon salt

8 whole wheat tortillas

2 cups grated Pepper Jack cheese

avocado slices

sour cream

## PICO DE GALLO:

2 cups quartered cherry tomatoes

2 tablespoons minced onion

2 teaspoons lime juice, freshly squeezed

¼ cup chopped cilantro

1 teaspoon minced jalapeño

½ teaspoon salt

# DIRECTIONS

1. *Mix together the ingredients for the pico de gallo, and set it aside to let the flavors blend together.*

2. *Heat a medium-size skillet over medium high heat. When the pan is hot, add the chorizo and sauté, breaking up the sausage with a spoon as it cooks. When the sausage is almost done, add the bell pepper, zucchini, mushrooms, corn, and sliced scallions. Cook until the veggies are crisp-tender, stirring often.*

3. *Whisk together the eggs and salt in a medium-size bowl. Then add them to the pan with the chorizo and veggies. Stir constantly as the eggs scramble. When the eggs are set, remove the pan from the heat.*

4. *Heat a separate skillet over medium heat. Lay one tortilla in the bottom of the skillet, and spread about ½ cup filling over the top. Sprinkle with cheese and top with a second tortilla. Cook until the cheese begins to melt and the bottom tortilla has turned golden brown. Carefully flip the quesadilla and cook on the other side until the cheese is molten and the second side is golden brown.*

5. *Repeat the cooking process with the remaining ingredients until you have 4 whole quesadillas, keeping them warm in the oven as you go.*

6. *Serve the hot quesadillas cut into wedges, with the pico de gallo, avocado slices, and sour cream.*

 **15** MIN *Prep Time*

 **20** MIN *Cook Time*

 **4** QUESADILLAS *Makes*

# BREAKFAST STRATA

If you follow me on any social media platform, then you've heard me talk (ad nauseam) about how imperative it is to plan out meals in advance. Anyone who's in on the make-ahead game can appreciate the strata for just this reason. If you're not familiar with it, imagine a sort of fancy bread pudding. This strata is the perfect make-ahead dish because you can create it on Sunday, let it rest overnight, and then enjoy it on Monday night for dinner. It's also a great option for when you're entertaining guests.

# INGREDIENTS

1 pound mild or hot Italian sausage

1 cup diced yellow onion

2 cups chopped baby spinach

2½ cups milk

2 teaspoons Zesty Italian seasoning

8 eggs

2½ teaspoons salt (or salt to taste based on your spice mix)

½ teaspoon black pepper

1 cup grated fontina cheese

1 cup grated Parmesan cheese

8 cups cubed bread, from 1 (2-ounce) baguette

2 cups halved cherry tomatoes

# DIRECTIONS

1. *Heat a large skillet over medium-high heat. When the pan is hot, add your choice of Italian sausage and the diced onion. Sauté while breaking up the sausage with a spoon. Cook until the sausage is cooked through and the onion has softened. Remove the pan from the heat and add the chopped spinach; stir the spinach in and let it wilt slightly as the pan cools.*

2. *Next, whisk together the milk, Zesty Italian seasoning, egg, salt, and black pepper until the eggs are completely blended into the milk. Stir in the fontina and Parmesan, and set the mixture aside.*

3. *Place the cubed bread into a 3½-quart baking dish, 12 x 8 x 3½ inches. Add the sausage spinach mixture and the halved cherry tomatoes, and stir to combine.*

4. *Pour the egg and cheese mixture evenly over the top of the bread cubes. Cover the dish and refrigerate 8 hours, or overnight.*

5. *When you're ready to bake the strata, preheat the oven to 350°F. When the oven is heated, place the baking dish in the oven and bake until the strata is golden brown, the eggs have set up, and it's puffed in the middle, about 1¼ hours.*

6. *Serve immediately.*

 *Prep Time* — 20 MIN

 *Cook Time* — 1¼ HOURS

8-10 SERVINGS *Makes*

## NOTES

1. *Strata must sit overnight to absorb the egg mixture, so it's a great make-ahead breakfast.*

2. *We used hot Italian sausage at Chic HQ.*

3. *Make sure your baking dish can go straight from the refrigerator to the oven.*

4. *The amount of salt needed may vary depending on which spice mix is used.*

5. *Artisan bread, like a baguette, gives the strata a better texture.*

# FREEZE-AHEAD BREAKFAST BURRITOS

This is a make-ahead winner and a great way to start your week. Whip up a bunch of burritos and get creative with your breakfast ingredients, then you can enjoy them for breakfast, lunch, or (our favorite!) dinner with only a quick dip in the microwave or oven.

# INGREDIENTS

2 tablespoons olive oil

1 bag frozen potatoes
(country hash browns)

12 large eggs, whisked with a splash
of milk (we used ½ cup in testing)

1 teaspoon salt

1 teaspoon black pepper

1 green bell pepper, diced

1 yellow bell pepper, diced

1 red bell pepper, diced

16 flour tortillas

8 slices bacon, cooked and
crumbled

1 cup breakfast sausage, cooked
and crumbled

2 cups shredded Cheddar cheese

*Serve with: salsa, sour cream, and
ripe avocado slices*

# DIRECTIONS

1. *Heat a large skillet over medium-high heat. Add the olive oil and allow to heat through. Throw in the potatoes and cook, stirring occasionally until browned. Add the eggs and cook until no longer runny. Season with salt and black pepper. Set aside.*

2. *Heat a small skillet over medium heat and sauté the bell peppers until soft.*

3. *Warm the tortillas on the stove in a dry skillet until pliable. Fill each one with the potato and egg mixture and top with bacon, sausage, peppers, and/or cheese.*

4. *Roll into a tight burrito. Wrap in foil and allow to cool down.*

5. *Store in the freezer and rewarm in the microwave (without the foil) or in a 350°F oven for 15 minutes before serving. Enjoy!*

**15** MIN — *Prep Time*

**25** MIN — *Cook Time*

**16** BURRITOS — *Makes*

# FREEZE-AHEAD BREAKFAST SANDWICHES

Let's be honest, you guys . . . if I wouldn't gain a thousand pounds by doing it, I would have McDonald's bacon, egg, and cheese biscuit for breakfast every day of my life. Sometimes I'd probably also have one as an afternoon snack. This recipe is my healthier at-home version. Sure, it doesn't come with that crispy hash brown, but it's pretty darn good and the fact that it's premade means it'll be so much easier to pull off when you are rushing out the door every morning.

## INGREDIENTS

Cooking spray

6 large eggs

6 English muffins, split in half

6 slices Cheddar cheese

### OPTIONAL FILLINGS:

Bacon, cooked until crispy

Sausage patties, cooked

Sliced ham

Canadian bacon

2 cups baby spinach

Honey mustard

Mayonnaise

## DIRECTIONS

1. Gather ingredients. Cook the eggs in a skillet with cooking spray, according to how you like them. Place on the bottoms of the English muffins and top with cheese.

2. Fill the sandwiches with desired toppings, if using, and then sandwich together. Wrap in wax or parchment paper and label for the week. Store in freezer until ready to eat.

3. To rewarm, unwrap sandwiches and place in a toaster oven, oven, or microwave. Cook for about 8 to 10 minutes in toaster oven or oven, or about 4 to 5 minutes in microwave.

 **20** MIN — *Prep Time*

 **10** MIN — *Cook Time* in the oven

 **4–5** MIN — *Cook Time* in the microwave

**6** SANDWICHES — *Makes*

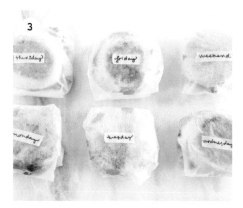

# SKILLET HUEVOS RANCHEROS

This shouldn't even be considered a breakfast recipe; this is brunch all the way. Imagine yourself sitting on the patio of a restaurant in Palm Springs with your best girlfriends. You've got a mimosa in your hand, or maybe one of those stacked Bloody Marys. What's on the menu today as you laugh and chat and live your best life? Huevos rancheros! Now, back in the reality of your kitchen, you can bring a little of that brunch fantasy into your everyday living. Mimosas are still strongly encouraged.

# INGREDIENTS

1 bunch scallions

2 tablespoons olive oil

1 garlic clove, minced

5 (5-inch) corn tortillas

1 (15-ounce) can pinto beans, rinsed and drained

1 tablespoon Rachel's Fiesta Blend

1 (14½-ounce) can crushed fire-roasted tomatoes

1 teaspoon salt

6 eggs

1½ cups grated Pepper Jack cheese

2 tablespoons chopped cilantro

1 ripe avocado, sliced

# DIRECTIONS

1. *Preheat the oven to 375°F, and thinly slice the scallions, both the white and green parts. Reserve the white and green parts separately.*

2. *Place a medium-size saucepan over medium-high heat, and add 1 tablespoon of the olive oil. When the oil is hot, add the garlic and the white part of the scallions. Sauté until the onion begins to soften, about 1 minute. Then add the pinto beans, Fiesta Blend, and fire-roasted tomatoes. Bring the mixture to a boil, then simmer for about 10 minutes before seasoning to taste with salt.*

3. *Add the remaining 1 tablespoon olive oil to a 9-inch cast-iron pan. Line the pan with the corn tortillas, making sure they come up the sides.*

4. *Spread the pinto bean mixture over the top of the tortillas, and make 6 indents in the bean mixture to hold the eggs. Scatter the reserved green part of the scallions over the beans. Crack the eggs open and add to the pan, spacing them evenly, and then top with grated cheese.*

5. *Place the skillet in the oven, and bake until the whites have set, about 15 minutes.*

6. *When the eggs are done, sprinkle with cilantro, and serve with avocado slices.*

 **10** MIN *Prep Time*

 **25** MIN *Cook Time*

 **4–6** SERVINGS *Makes*

# SOUTHWESTERN BREAKFAST SCRAMBLE

Real talk: when we taste-tested this recipe at the office, I nearly peed my pants because it was mind-blowingly good. Also, it was the first time I'd tried out my new line of spices in a real-life recipe. I'm so proud of the results and so proud that you'll get to try my favorite flavors (and recipes) in your own kitchen. Olé!

# INGREDIENTS

6 eggs

½ teaspoon salt

1 to 2 teaspoons olive oil

2 cups thinly sliced bell peppers

½ cup corn, frozen or canned

½ cup thinly sliced scallions

½ cup canned black beans, rinsed and drained

1 teaspoon Fiesta Blend

½ cup grated Pepper Jack cheese

## PICO DE GALLO:

1½ cups chopped cherry tomatoes

2 tablespoons chopped cilantro

2 tablespoons onion, finely diced

1 teaspoon minced jalapeño

1 teaspoon lime juice, freshly squeezed

¼ teaspoon salt

Serve with: avocado slices and sour cream

# DIRECTIONS

1. *Mix together all the ingredients for the pico de gallo, and set it aside to let the flavors develop.*

2. *Whisk together the eggs and salt, and set the mixture aside.*

3. *Preheat a medium-size skillet over medium-high heat. When the pan is hot, add 1 teaspoon of the olive oil, along with the bell pepper. Sauté until the bell pepper slices are just tender, 3 to 4 minutes.*

4. *Then add the corn, scallions, black beans, and Fiesta Blend to the pan. Cook, stirring until the ingredients are hot, then add the egg mixture and stir constantly as the eggs scramble.*

5. *When the eggs are almost set, add the Pepper Jack cheese, and stir until the eggs are done and the cheese is melted.*

6. *Serve the eggs with pico de gallo, avocado slices, and sour cream.*

 **20** MIN *Prep Time*

 **10** MIN *Cook Time*

 **4** SERVINGS *Makes*

## NOTES

*I used a mixture of red, yellow, and green bell peppers for this recipe for the pretty colors.*

# TWICE-BAKED BACON AND EGG POTATOES

Back when I was a young adult (and I use the word "adult" loosely) living in L.A., I couldn't afford to go out to eat—unless you count my weekly splurge at Subway— but every once in a while I'd treat myself to dinner at the Daily Grill. The Daily Grill is an L.A. institution, and at the time it was way more expensive than I could actually afford. But like every scrappy (read: poor) young woman, I got really creative with house bread, water, and the "sides" menu. I had never had a twice-baked potato before my first trip to that restaurant, but it quickly became one of my favorite splurges. This recipe is a little decadent, but with an egg on top so you feel better about your life choices.

# INGREDIENTS

2 teaspoons olive oil

3 large russet potatoes, washed

¾ cup Greek yogurt

½ cup buttermilk

1 tablespoon Southwestern Ranch seasoning

½ cup thinly sliced scallions

1 teaspoon salt

½ teaspoon black pepper

6 strips bacon, cooked and crumbled

1½ cups grated Cheddar cheese

6 eggs

# DIRECTIONS

1. Preheat the oven to 400°F, and rub the olive oil over the potatoes to evenly coat the skins. Prick the potatoes a couple of times with a fork, and place them on a baking sheet. Bake the potatoes for 1 hour, or until they're soft in the middle.

2. Remove the potatoes from the oven, and let them cool slightly. Using oven mitts to protect your hands, slice the potatoes in half lengthwise, and scoop out the middle of the potatoes into a bowl. Leave a little potato around the edges of the potato skins to help them hold their shape.

3. Add the Greek yogurt, buttermilk, Southwestern Ranch seasoning, scallions, salt, and black pepper to the bowl with the scooped-out potato. Mash it all together until the potato mixture is smooth. Then stir in the bacon and 1 cup of the Cheddar cheese.

4. Spoon the filling back into the potato skins, making a 1-inch deep well in the middle of each potato to hold the egg. You can refrigerate the potatoes at this point for up to 2 days, and bake later if desired. Just add the egg right before baking, sprinkle with the remaining cheese, and bake until the egg whites have set, about 40 minutes.

5. To bake right away, add an egg into each well of the 6 potato halves, and transfer them to a parchment-lined baking sheet.

6. Sprinkle with the remaining ½ cup cheese, and bake the potatoes until the egg whites have set and the cheese is bubbly, about 20 to 25 minutes.

 **20** MIN *Prep Time*

 **1.5** HOURS *Cook Time*

 **6** SERVINGS *Makes*

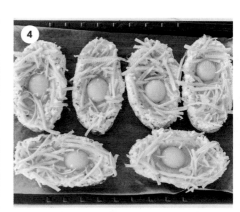

# TOAST 9 WAYS

I'm trying to figure out if there's any easier, more versatile option for a light dinner than toast. No. There's definitely not. It's such an easy way to use up what's in your fridge or pantry, or you can go the extra mile and use cool ingredients to mix it up a little. My all-time favorite is avocado toast, but if you need some inspiration for your own new favorite, try out one of these nine recipes.

# INGREDIENTS

*Slices of multigrain bread* (toasted)

# TOPPINGS

1. *Smashed avocado, sliced radishes, chopped cilantro, crumbled cojita cheese, and cucumber*

2. *Cherry jam, Black Forest ham, and sliced brie cheese*

3. *Ricotta, prosciutto, cantaloupe, and honey*

4. *Cream cheese mashed with blueberries, topped with sliced strawberries*

5. *Mascarpone, sliced plums, pumpkin seeds, and honey*

6. *Ricotta, sliced pears, and honey*

7. *Peanut butter, sliced banana, and honey*

8. *Cream cheese, cucumber, olive oil, salt, black pepper, and red pepper flakes*

9. *Hummus, sliced sweet peppers, and crumbled feta cheese*

 *Prep Time* — 10 MIN

 *Cook Time* — 5 MIN

*Makes* — ∞ SERVINGS

# KID-FRIENDLY DINNERS

Kids? Am-I-right?

Can't live with 'em, can't legally sell them to a traveling circus.

Seriously, though, being a parent is so hard.

Don't get me wrong, it's awesome on a thousand different levels, but it's also terrifying. Anyone else remember leaving the hospital with your first baby, thinking, *Blessed Redeemer, why would you trust me with a whole human being?*

The first time the pediatrician asked me if my toddler had been to the dentist yet, I started crying. I figured he wouldn't need to see a dentist until he had permanent choppers, and the reality that he needed to go as a two-year-old was almost too much to bear. I just kept thinking, *I can barely remember to brush my own teeth and now I have to be responsible for his dental hygiene along with everything else??*

Then there's what to feed them.

When you have babies, figuring out what to feed them is basically the easiest part of your entire parenting career. But when they get older? All bets are off. In the house I grew up in, you ate whatever my mama served. Period. But when I tried that with my kids, they rebelled, stopped eating altogether or—for my particularly gaggy toddler—literally threw it up all over the dining room table.

Are you serious?! Where is that written in the life manual? Where is that chapter in *What To Expect When You're Expecting*? It doesn't exist, probably because if it did, we might think twice about how capable we are of keeping other humans alive.

No mind, though. I turned to books to try and learn how to feed them. I read every single one on convincing my kids to eat and fully bought into the principles in each. Those books described a euphoric future dinner where my children would inhale spinach and pureed carrots with glee.

Imagine how utterly dismayed I was when it didn't work.

Basically, if it wasn't Cheerios or grapes, they weren't interested. But I wasn't interested in creating separate dinners for the adults and children in our house. I finally decided to figure out what would work for *my kids,* not the fictional cherubs in those books who love pureed beets.

It was slow going.

Any parent who's ever worked hard on a dinner only to have a four-year-old scream that he'd rather have a PB&J can understand my pain. Over the last several years I've decided not to fight them on the things they refuse to eat, but rather just figure out some real-life workarounds that, well, work for us all. Sometimes that means reinventing the food they love in healthier ways, other times it's about getting them involved in the process so they're more likely to eat what's on the table. It's a lot of trial and error, a lot of putting the same ingredient on their plate again and again and again until they're not afraid of it. It's also a lot of repeat meals, because they are creatures of habit and once I figure out what they like, I exploit it for all it's worth! Here are some of our favorites.

# BISCUIT PIZZA

I grew up in a house that always had a tin of biscuits in the refrigerator. Mama would use them as a side dish for dinner or as the base for breakfast on Saturday morning. You can use them to make pigs in a blanket or mini calzones, but my kids' absolute favorite is to use biscuits as the base for individual pizzas. When you roll out a biscuit, it is the perfect size for a child to create their own pie. This is a great option for easy weeknight dinners (because a jar of pizza sauce lasts forever in the fridge, and we always have cheese on hand). It's also a fun activity for a play date. Set the kids up with toppings and then let them go to town.

# INGREDIENTS

Cooking spray

1 can (8-count) biscuits

1 jar pizza sauce

2 cups grated mozzarella cheese

## OPTIONAL TOPPINGS:

1 package sliced pepperoni

2 to 4 slices Canadian bacon

¼ cup pineapple tidbits

¼ to ½ cup black olives

2 to 4 slices green bell pepper

# DIRECTIONS

1. *Preheat the oven to 375°F and lightly spray 2 baking sheets with cooking spray.*

2. *Pat out each biscuit into a ½-inch thick circle, about 6 inches across (you can fit 4 per baking sheet).*

3. *Spread a small amount (about 1 tablespoon) of pizza sauce per biscuit.*

*Then top each pizza individually with cheese and your choice of toppings, if using.*

4. *Bake each baking sheet for 12 to 15 minutes, or until the biscuit is fully cooked, and the cheese is bubbling.*

5. *Serve immediately.*

**15** MIN *Prep Time*

**15** MIN *Cook Time*

**8** PIZZAS *Makes*

# HOMEMADE HOT POCKETS

Let's get real, you guys—you could wrap almost anything in puff pastry and it would be delicious! In this instance we used the superstar pastry to make my kids the kind of thing they beg for from the freezer aisle at the supermarket but I refuse to buy: Hot Pockets. We made ham and cheese, but you can experiment to create your own favorite flavors.

# INGREDIENTS

Cooking spray

1 package (17.3-ounce) frozen puff pastry, thawed

2 tablespoons honey mustard

12 slices deli ham

1 cup grated cheese, fontina or Cheddar

1 egg, lightly beaten

1 teaspoon Zesty Italian seasoning

½ cup grated Parmesan cheese

# DIRECTIONS

1. Preheat the oven to 375°F and lightly spray 2 baking sheets with cooking spray.

2. Unwrap the puff pastry and cut each sheet into 3 long strips following along the fold lines, for a total of 6 rectangles.

3. Using a rolling pin, roll each rectangle into 12-inch lengths. Spread about 1 teaspoon of honey mustard along each half of the 6 rectangles, leaving a ½-inch space around the edges.

4. Fold each slice of ham into a rectangle, and place 2 slices of ham per pastry on one end. Top each ham slice with about 2 tablespoons of grated cheese.

5. Brush the edges with the beaten egg, and fold the pastry in half, pressing around the edges to seal the pastries. Then using a fork, lightly crimp the edges.

6. Repeat with the remaining 5 pastries, transferring each to the baking sheets as you go.

7. Lightly brush the beaten egg over the pastries, and sprinkle with Zesty Italian seasoning, and Parmesan cheese.

8. Bake each pan of pastries for 15 to 18 minutes, or until golden brown and crispy.

 **20** MIN  Prep Time

 **15** MIN  Cook Time

 **6** POCKETS  Makes

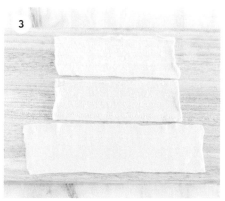

3

5

# SUB SANDWICH

My very first real job was at a sandwich shop and I *loved* it. I loved it there because (1) I got to eat for free and sandwiches are delicious and (2) in the afternoon when I was there alone, I would read *People* magazines in between customers. Free food plus catching up on that week's Mailbag made it one of the best jobs I've ever had. It also made me a near expert on the creation of a good sub sandwich, which is why I started making this big Dagwood for my kids' birthday parties years ago. It's a great option because you can make it basic (just the meat and the cheese) and then leave the fixings on the side so guests can make their own version, or go full tilt like I do and force everyone to enjoy a sub as God intended . . . with *everything* on it.

# INGREDIENTS

2 loaves French bread, 1 pound each

¼ cup mayonnaise

¼ cup honey mustard

3 pounds sliced smoked turkey

1 pound sliced provolone cheese

½ pound sliced Cheddar cheese

1 red onion, thinly sliced

1 small head romaine, washed
and finely shredded

8 tomatoes, thinly sliced

## SUBMARINE DRESSING:

½ cup olive oil

¼ cup white wine vinegar

2 teaspoons Zesty Italian seasoning

½ teaspoon salt

1 teaspoon honey mustard

# DIRECTIONS

**1.** *Add all the Submarine Dressing ingredients to a jar or squeeze bottle. Secure the lid and shake the dressing together to emulsify. Set it aside to let the flavors blend while you make the sandwich.*

**2.** *Split both French breads in half lengthwise, and spread them evenly with the mayonnaise and mustard.*

**3.** *Evenly divide the turkey and cheeses between the 2 sandwiches. Top with the red onion, tomatoes, and shredded romaine.*

**4.** *Drizzle the submarine dressing over both sides of each sandwich. Then place the tops on each sandwich, slice, and serve.*

**30** MIN *Prep Time*

**12** SERVINGS *Makes*

# TACO TUESDAY

A make-your-own taco bar is the perfect dinner to serve when you have a family coming over that has kids . . . it's my go-to! Because kids can be picky eaters and other people's children are even harder to feed because you have no idea what they like, a meal like this allows people to pick and choose. And you know how it goes, right? Your friends are going to make a burrito the size of an economy car, and then their five-year-old is going to want lettuce and a tortilla only. You can feel good that you did your job, you gave Chloe tens of options and she went minimalist. That's not on you, your tacos were delicious!

# INGREDIENTS

4 tomatoes, chopped

2 cups grated Cheddar cheese

1 romaine heart, washed and finely shredded

½ to ¾ cup sour cream

1 pound ground beef

1 package taco seasoning

12 small flour tortillas

## ADDITIONAL TACO TOPPINGS:

Avocado, salsa, guacamole, beans, corn—basically, if they serve it at Chipotle, you should totally consider adding it to your taco bar!

# DIRECTIONS

1. *Prep the tomatoes, romaine, cheese, and sour cream. Set them aside in serving bowls while you finish the recipe.*

2. *Place a 9-inch skillet over medium-high heat. When the pan is hot, add the ground beef and cook, breaking it up with a wooden spoon until it's no longer pink. Add the taco seasoning and cook for another 15 minutes to let the flavors develop.*

3. *Heat up the tortillas briefly in a skillet or in the oven for a couple minutes.*

4. *Serve the taco meat with the warm tortillas and toppings.*

**20** MIN *Prep Time*

**20** MIN *Cook Time*

**4** SERVINGS *Makes*

# MEAT LOAF MEATBALLS

Have I told you guys how much I love meat loaf? I really, really love it. A good meat loaf with mashed potatoes and corn is one of my top five dream meals, so it's no surprise that I'm constantly trying to convince my kids to try one of my childhood favorites. It took me a minute to figure out how to get them to eat meat loaf, but here are my tried-and-true tricks. First of all, fill the meatballs with veggies but make sure the veggies aren't super obvious. If I were making this for you and me, you'd see all the yummy produce you were getting, but since this is for my kids, I'll chop the items to make them smaller. Speaking of smaller, creating bite-size food is often how I'll get them to give something a go. The added bonus here is that these meatballs cook in way less time than an actual meat loaf.

# INGREDIENTS

Cooking spray

⅔ cup rolled oats

1 cup roughly chopped onion

1 cup sliced carrots

1 ½ cup roughly chopped zucchini

1 pound ground beef

1 egg

¼ cup ketchup or barbecue sauce

1 teaspoon salt

½ teaspoon black pepper

½ cup ketchup or barbecue sauce for brushing

# DIRECTIONS

1. *Preheat the oven to 400°F and lightly spray 2 baking sheets with cooking spray.*

2. *Place the rolled oats, onion, carrots, and zucchini into a food processor and process until a chunky mixture forms with small pieces no bigger than ¼ inch.*

3. *Mix together the oat mixture, ground beef, egg, ketchup or barbecue sauce, salt, and black pepper until thoroughly combined.*

4. *Roll the mixture until meatballs form, and place them on the baking sheet. You will have about 36 meatballs, using 2 tablespoons of the meatball mixture for each.*

5. *Brush the tops of the meatballs with your choice of ketchup or barbecue sauce, and bake until the edges are browned and the meatballs are done in the center, 15 to 18 minutes.*

6. *Repeat with the second baking sheet, and serve immediately. You can also bake both baking sheets at the same time, rotating them in the oven halfway through the cooking time.*

 **20** MIN — *Prep Time*

 **15** MIN — *Cook Time*

 **4–6** SERVINGS — *Makes*

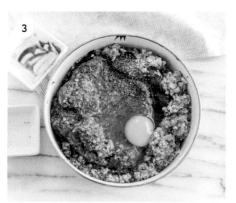

# PINEAPPLE CHICKEN STIR-FRY

This was the most common dinner served in our home growing up. We had it at least once a week, and for some reason my mom always served it with garlic bread. It makes no real sense to serve stir-fry with a giant loaf of sourdough, but then, our family often leaned heavily into carbs and this dinner was no exception. Nowadays I like making it with chicken and cauliflower (the boys eat the chicken, I eat the cauliflower), and it can be served over steamed rice or on top of mixed greens. This is also one of those dishes where the leftovers are almost as good as the main course, so consider doubling the recipe to enjoy later in the week for lunch.

# INGREDIENTS

1 yellow onion, diced ½ inch thick

2 cups pineapple chunks

1 red bell pepper, diced ½ inch thick

1 green bell pepper, diced ½ inch thick

2 garlic cloves, minced

1 tablespoon minced fresh ginger

¼ cup soy sauce

1 teaspoon cornstarch

¼ cup water

2 boneless, skinless chicken breasts (1 pound)

1 to 2 tablespoons cooking oil

½ cup thinly sliced scallions

# DIRECTIONS

1. *Prep the veggies and fruit and set them aside. Prep the garlic and ginger, and set them aside in a small bowl.*

2. *Make the stir-fry sauce by mixing together the soy sauce and cornstarch until no lumps remain. Whisk in the water and set the sauce aside.*

3. *Preheat a large (12- to 15-inch) skillet over medium heat, and cut the chicken up into 1-inch pieces.*

4. *When the skillet is hot, add 1 tablespoon of the cooking oil to the pan along with the chicken. Turn the heat to high, and sauté until the chicken is browned and almost cooked through, 4 to 5 minutes.*

5. *Remove the chicken from the pan, and add the onion, pineapple, scallions, and red and green pepper. Cook, stirring often until the veggies are crisp-tender, 3 to 4 minutes, adding the additional tablespoon of olive oil if necessary.*

6. *Add the chicken back to the pan along with the garlic and ginger, stir-fry until just fragrant, about 30 seconds. Then add the stir-fry sauce, and lower the heat to medium. Cook until the sauce thickens and the chicken is completely cooked through, about 1 minute.*

 **20** MIN *Prep Time*

 **10** MIN *Cook Time*

 **4** SERVINGS *Makes*

# SIMPLE GRILLED STEAK

I discovered this particular dish when I was trying to figure out what kinds of protein my boys would actually eat. They were interested in eating steak, but if I tried to season it how I like to eat it (which is to say, throw every single herb I've got into the mix), it was like I'd tried to poison them. My solution? I get a couple of great pieces of meat and season both of them with just three simple ingredients . . . then I add a little extra kick to the piece for Dave before grilling. This is Ford Hollis's favorite entrée ever.

# INGREDIENTS

¼ teaspoon salt

¼ teaspoon black pepper

Pinch of garlic powder (⅛ teaspoon)

1 large steak, 1 ½ pound (rib eye, New York, or sirloin)

# DIRECTIONS

1. *Preheat a grill over medium-high heat until the grill reaches a steady temperature between 400° and 450°F.*

2. *Mix together the salt, black pepper, and garlic powder in a small bowl. Season the steak evenly on both sides with the salt mixture.*

3. *Grill the steak, about 8 to 10 minutes per side for a 2-inch-thick steak done to medium.*

4. *Let the steak rest on a serving platter for 5 to 10 minutes before serving.*

 *Prep Time* — **5** MIN

 *Cook Time* — **15-20** MIN

 *Makes* — **4** SERVINGS

# BAKED RAVIOLI

Sometimes I need as much help as I can get to have dinner on the table after a long day at work. And sister, the last thing we want to do is spend the entire evening in the kitchen which is where I came up with meals that you could cheat a little. My Baked Ravioli is the jam because I start with pre-made ravioli and doctor them up to be a little more exciting.

# INGREDIENTS

1 tablespoon olive oil

2 bags frozen ravioli

1 (24-ounce) jar marinara sauce

¼ cup bread crumbs

1 (16-ounce) fresh mozzarella log, thinly sliced

fresh basil leaves

# DIRECTIONS

1. Preheat oven to 350° F. Grease a 9x13-inch baking dish with the olive oil and set aside.

2. Bring a large pot of cold water to a boil and season with salt. Add the ravioli and cook according to package directions, removing it a few minutes earlier since it'll continue to cook in the oven. Drain and return to pot. Toss the ravioli with marinara and pour half of it into the prepared dish. Spread out into an even layer. Sprinkle with half of the bread crumbs and top with half of the cheese slices. Tear a few basil leaves and sprinkle on top. Place the remaining ravioli on top, spreading it out into an even layer and top with remaining bread crumbs and cheese slices.

3. Bake for about 25 to 30 minutes or until bubbly and golden brown. You can place it under the broiler for a few seconds to brown the top. Remove from oven and garnish with a few basil leaves before serving.

**10 MIN** Prep Time

**30 MIN** Cook Time

**6 SERVINGS** Makes

# ONE-POT CHICKEN AND MEXICAN RICE

As a newlywed there were very few dishes I could actually cook well.

One dish I mastered was the turkey chili I shared with you in my first cookbook, and the other was One-Pot Chicken and Mexican Rice. Granted, when I was making this, I might have been using a box of Rice-A-Roni, but I did doctor it up with black beans and corn and enough sour cream to sink a small sailboat. Dave and I were huge fans of this dinner back in the day, and now it's a yummy weekend treat as a grown-up version.

# INGREDIENTS

6 boneless, skinless chicken thighs (about 1 ½ pounds)

1 teaspoon salt

1 teaspoon black pepper

½ teaspoon cumin

½ teaspoon dried oregano

¼ teaspoon cayenne

1 lime, juiced

2 tablespoons olive oil

1 small yellow onion, diced

2 garlic cloves, minced

1 red bell pepper, diced

1 cup long-grain white rice

1 cup frozen corn

1 (14-ounce) can black beans, drained

1 small can green chiles

1 cup chicken stock or broth

¾ cup tomato sauce

# DIRECTIONS

1. *In a medium bowl, combine the chicken, salt, black pepper, cumin, oregano, cayenne, and lime juice. Allow to marinate for about 30 minutes.*

2. *Set a large skillet over medium-high heat with the olive oil. Sear the chicken on both sides until browned. You're not cooking it all the way—just getting the brown color and flavor. Transfer to a plate and set aside. In the same skillet,* *add the onions, garlic, bell peppers, rice, corn, black beans, and green chiles. Sauté for about 8 minutes. Stir in the broth and tomato sauce and add the chicken, tucking it into the rice and veggies. Cover, lower the heat to low, and cook until the liquid is absorbed and the rice is tender and fluffy.*

3. *Serve with chips, sour cream, red bell pepper, and cheese.*

 **15** MIN *Prep Time*

 **30** MIN *Cook Time*

**6** SERVINGS *Makes*

# ITALIAN DRESSING GRILLED CHICKEN

I have been marinating my grilled chicken in Zesty Italian dressing since Girl Scout camp in the sixth grade. Technically, I wasn't doing the marinating back then, but the first time I had Italian dressing-grilled chicken was the same trip where we performed a choreographed dance to "Indian Outlaw" by Tim McGraw— so the memory is still fresh in my mind. I still use Zesty Italian dressing to marinate my own chicken because it adds such wonderful flavor. I typically find that bottled marinades at the store are too salty or too tangy, but Italian dressing gives it just the right amount of seasoning.

## INGREDIENTS

3 pounds boneless, skinless chicken breasts

1 bottle Zesty Italian dressing

Olive oil or cooking spray, for greasing

1 to 1 ½ cups barbecue sauce

## DIRECTIONS

1. Place the chicken in a large Ziplock bag. Pour the dressing over it and seal the bag tightly. Shake everything together, using your hands to make sure the chicken is fully coated. Place on a plate or bowl and chill in the fridge overnight.

2. Heat a stovetop or outdoor grill over medium-high heat. Grease with a bit of oil or cooking spray. Drain most of the dressing off each piece, then carefully place the chicken on the hot grill. Cook for about 3 to 4 minutes on the first side.

Flip over and cook for 2 to 3 minutes on the second side. Brush the chicken with barbecue sauce and flip over. Continue to brush each side with barbecue sauce, flipping and cooking for about 10 minutes. You'll know the chicken is done when the internal temperature reads 165°F with a cooking thermometer.

3. Transfer to a plate or platter and cover loosely with foil. Allow to sit about 10 to 15 minutes before slicing and serving.

 **24** HOURS *Prep Time*

 **20** MIN *Cook Time*

 **8** SERVINGS *Makes*

# MAKE-AHEAD DINNERS

Be prepared. It's the Boy Scout motto, and I may have referenced it one way or another in every single book I've written. I continue to shout this adage atop every platform because being prepared is how I'm able to juggle a hectic life and still feel relatively calm. If you want to do anything well in life, you have to prep for it. So if the goal is getting dinner on the table for yourself or your family while managing their crazy schedules and your own, the best advice I can offer you is meal prep. Prepping your meals in advance will always get you something delicious without much effort.

In our house, Sunday has become the designated meal-prep day for several reasons. After church we come home and settle in for the afternoon, and I use the opportunity to make a list of what I want to prep for the week. My prep menu is always based on the calendar week ahead. Do I have a lot of lunch meetings? Then there's no reason to prep lunches. Do I have some early

workouts? It's probably a good idea to create some overnight oatmeal so I can get breakfast in a hurry. Do we have company for dinner on Thursday? Then I need to prep a dinner that's twice the normal size and extra tasty.

All of these recipes are dishes that can be prepped and frozen to thaw and cook later . . . or they're good to go for dinner tonight if you just want something yummy and don't have time to plan ahead. By taking the time to prep these in the freezer, you'll have tons of great options to choose from during the week. Just pull out the dish in the morning, allow it to defrost in the fridge all day, and pop it in the oven when you're ready to eat.

Now you're free to focus on the week ahead instead of stressing about what you're going to make for dinner each night.

# DR PEPPER PULLED PORK

Let's face it—I may live in Los Angeles now, but I'm still a downhome girl who loves me some Dr Pepper and some sweet and savory pulled pork. This recipe instantly makes my mouth water. It's a family favorite and sure to get my boys to the table in a hurry. The best part about this recipe is that it's perfect for your slow cooker, so it makes an easy dish for our annual Super Bowl party or even for a festive Tuesday. The pulled pork can be made in advance, but hold off on making the coleslaw until the day you serve this delectable dish. Coleslaw does not freeze well.

# INGREDIENTS

1 boneless pork shoulder (5 to 6 pounds)

2 tablespoons all-purpose pork grilling rub

1 can Dr Pepper

1 cup barbecue sauce

Serve with: butter-toasted buns, coleslaw (recipe is below)

# DIRECTIONS

## PULLED PORK

1. *Rub the pork shoulder on all sides with the seasoning, and place it in a slow cooker.*

2. *Pour the can of Dr Pepper over the top.*

3. *Cover, and turn the slow cooker on high for 6 to 8 hours, or until the meat is tender and falling apart.*

4. *Carefully remove the pork from the cooking liquid, and place it on a platter or cutting board to cool.*

5. *Pour the cooking liquid out of the slow cooker into a bowl and reserve it.*

6. *Shred the pork and place it back into the slow cooker, then add 1 cup of the reserved cooking liquid and the barbecue sauce.*

7. *Stir to combine, and cook the pork on high for another 30 minutes, checking at the halfway point to see if you need to add a bit more of the reserved cooking liquid.*

8. *Freeze the extra pulled pork in 2- to 4-cup packages, remove all the air from the container, and freeze to use within 1 to 3 months.*

 *Prep Time*

 *Cook Time*

 *Makes*

## COLESLAW
# INGREDIENTS

4 cups finely shredded purple cabbage

1 cup grated carrots

½ cup thinly sliced scallions

½ cup mayonnaise

2 tablespoons freshly squeezed lemon juice

2 teaspoons sugar

½ teaspoon salt

# DIRECTIONS

1. *Toss the cabbage, carrots, and scallions together in a medium-size bowl.*

2. *Mix together the mayonnaise, lemon juice, sugar, and salt until completely smooth.*

3. *Combine the slaw and dressing together right before serving.*

 *Prep Time*

 *Makes*

# HOMEMADE FROZEN BURRITOS

When I was little, my parents used to get frozen burritos from Costco by the boatload. Those delicious little burritos were half my diet in junior high (which would explain all the extra fluff I carried around back then), and I absolutely loved them. Offer me doughnuts or a frosted cupcake and I can show some small semblance of self-control (although I beg of you not to challenge me, 'cause I'm still only human), but when faced with an endless chip basket and a burrito at any Mexican restaurant, I lose my mind. It's like a chips-and-salsa spell has been cast on me. So when I was coming up with some of our favorite dinnertime go-tos, I couldn't help but include my cherished frozen burrito recipe. Stock your freezer with these burritos for a meal that's healthier and way easier on your wallet.

# INGREDIENTS

1 cup long-grain white rice

1 tablespoon olive oil

1 onion, diced

1 garlic clove, minced

1 pound ground beef

1 tablespoon Fiesta Blend

1 (15-ounce) can pinto beans, rinsed

1½ cups salsa

Salt

10 burrito-sized (10-inch) tortillas

3 cups grated cheese, Pepper Jack or Monterey Jack

*Serve with: sour cream, salsa, avocado, cilantro, and sliced scallions*

# DIRECTIONS

1. *Rinse the rice with water, drain, and place it in a medium-size saucepan. Cover the rice with 1½ cups water, and bring it to a boil. Then reduce the heat to low, cover the pan, and cook until all the liquid has been absorbed and the rice is tender, about 20 minutes.*

2. *Meanwhile, heat a large skillet over medium-high heat. When the pan is hot, add the oil and diced onion. Cook until the onion is tender and slightly translucent, about 5 minutes. Then add the garlic and ground beef. Continue to cook, breaking up the ground beef as you go, until the beef is no longer pink. Then add the Fiesta Blend, pinto beans, and salsa, stirring to combine. Remove the pan from the heat, and set it aside.*

3. *When the rice is done, stir it into the beef-and-bean mixture until thoroughly combined. Season to taste with salt.*

4. *To assemble the burritos, lay a tortilla on the counter and sprinkle ¼ to ⅓ cup of cheese on each. Add 1 cup of the beef-and-bean filling, and roll the burrito up, tucking in the ends before wrapping it in foil. Repeat the process until all 10 burritos are assembled and wrapped.*

5. *Place the wrapped burritos in an airtight container and freeze for up to 1 month.*

6. *To cook the burritos, remove them from the freezer the night before, and thaw in the refrigerator. Preheat an oven to 375°F and bake until the burritos are hot in the center, 20 to 25 minutes. Serve with your choice of toppings.*

 **20** MIN *Prep Time*

 **40** MIN *Cook Time*

 **10** BURRITOS *Makes*

# HAWAIIAN CHICKEN

Have I told you about my vacation home in Hawaii? Okay, I don't actually own one . . . yet. But it's a big part of my life plan. Hawaii is possibly my favorite place on earth. There's something in the air and in the water that is soothing to my soul. If you've been there before, I'm guessing you know exactly what I mean. Several trips ago I mentioned to my darling husband that I wished we owned a vacation home there. To which Mr. Pragmatic said that it didn't make sense because L.A. is a five-hour flight away from Hawaii. Just to give you the whole picture, we don't have the money to buy a vacation home *anywhere* let alone on a Hawaiian island. I was simply daydreaming over wine at dinner, and he was being a spoilsport. So I threw down the gauntlet. I was going to own a vacation home in Hawaii, and he'd have to ask me, *very nicely,* if he ever wanted to use it. Our kids got in on it, too. My oldest said he'd love to come to Hawaii with me. Our middle son—the traitor—said he'd prefer to stay with Daddy back in California. The four-year-old ignored us all while blowing bubbles in his milk with a straw. The point of all of this is that now whenever we talk about Hawaii, we always talk about my future vacation home there, and while we wait, I make dishes like this Hawaiian Chicken to keep the dream alive.

## INGREDIENTS

1 red bell pepper, diced into 1-inch pieces

1 cup diced onion

Serve with: ½ cup thinly sliced scallions

1½ cups pineapple chunks

1 tablespoon minced ginger

2 garlic cloves, minced

4 boneless, skinless chicken breasts, (about 2 pounds) cut into 1-inch pieces

2 tablespoons cornstarch

½ cup soy sauce

¼ cup ketchup

¼ cup honey or brown sugar

## DIRECTIONS

1. Place the bell pepper, onion, pineapple chunks, ginger, garlic, and chicken into a gallon freezer ziplock bag.

2. In a small bowl, stir together the cornstarch and soy sauce until no lumps remain. Add the ketchup and honey (or brown sugar, if using), and stir until completely combined. If your honey isn't in a liquid state, briefly heat it before whisking it in.

3. Pour the sauce into the ziplock bag with the chicken mixture. Seal the bag and, using your hands, lightly mix the contents together.

4. You can cook the chicken right away, or remove all air from the bag and freeze for later use.

5. When you're ready to use your freezer meal, remove the bag from the freezer the night before and thaw it in the fridge.

6. Place the thawed Hawaiian Chicken into a slow cooker, and cook on high for 2 hours, or low for 4 hours, or until the chicken is cooked through and the sauce has thickened. Start checking the chicken before the end of the cooking time, as every slow cooker is different.

7. Leftovers freeze well.

 **20** MIN *Prep Time*

 **2** HOURS *Cook Time*

**6** SERVINGS *Makes*

# MEXICAN CASSEROLE

This is sort of like a lasagna, only instead of noodles and red sauce we're putting a little Latin spin on it! Combining my two passions, Mexican food and casseroles, felt like a total no-brainer when I was gathering recipes that were easy to create, tasty, and freezer friendly. I wanted something that was delicious when you heat it up yet still easy to make in advance. This recipe definitely checks off those boxes.

# INGREDIENTS

2 tablespoons olive oil

2 boneless, skinless chicken breasts (1 pound), cut into 1-inch pieces

½ medium onion, diced

1 red bell pepper, diced

1 green bell pepper, diced

1 tablespoon Fiesta Blend

1 teaspoon ground cumin

1 cup frozen corn

1 (15-ounce) can black beans, rinsed

1 (14½-ounce) can fire-roasted tomatoes with green chiles

1½ teaspoons salt

10 to 12 (5-inch) corn tortillas

2 cups grated Pepper Jack cheese

Serve with: sour cream and guacamole

# DIRECTIONS

1. Preheat oven to 400°F and lightly grease a 9 by 12-inch baking dish.

2. Place a large skillet over medium-high heat. When the pan is hot, add 1 tablespoon of the olive oil, along with the cubed chicken. Sauté until the chicken is browned and cooked through. Remove the chicken from the pan and set it aside.

3. In the same skillet, add the remaining tablespoon of olive oil along with the onion and both bell peppers. Cook until the vegetables are crisp-tender, about 5 minutes. Then add the Fiesta Blend, cumin, corn, black beans, fire-roasted tomatoes with green chiles, and cooked chicken to the pan. Cook just until the mixture is hot, 1 to 2 minutes. Season to taste with salt.

4. Cut the corn tortillas into 4 equal strips. Start layering the casserole by covering the bottom of the baking dish with tortilla strips, then spoon half of the chicken-and-veggie mixture evenly over the tortilla strips. Top with half of the grated cheese, then add another layer of tortilla strips and filling. Top the filling with the remaining tortilla strips and sprinkle with the remaining cup of cheese.

5. Bake until the casserole is browned on top and bubbling around the edges, 25 to 30 minutes.

6. Serve immediately with your choice of toppings, or let the casserole cool, cover it tightly, and freeze to use within 1 month. Thaw the casserole overnight in the fridge before reheating at 300°F.

 **20** MIN *Prep Time*

 **40** MIN *Cook Time*

 **6** SERVINGS *Makes*

# CHICKEN POTPIE

Let's get real. Chicken Potpie is the food that would hug you if it could. It's the ultimate comfort food, which makes this the perfect recipe to prep in advance for a new mama. Make a couple for your freezer and a couple for hers and drop it off with baking instructions so she doesn't have to think through dinner while trying to keep a new baby (and herself!) alive.

# INGREDIENTS

6 tablespoons butter

2 boneless, skinless chicken breasts, (about 1 pound) cut into 1-inch pieces

1 cup diced onion

1 cup thinly sliced carrots

½ cup thinly sliced celery

1 garlic clove, minced

2 teaspoons minced fresh thyme, or ½ teaspoon dried thyme

⅓ cup all-purpose flour

1 ½ cups chicken stock

¾ cup half-and-half

1 teaspoon salt

½ teaspoon black pepper

1 cup frozen peas

1 package premade pie crust (two 9-inch crusts), brought to room temperature

1 egg

# DIRECTIONS

1. Preheat the oven to 350°F.

2. Place a medium-size saucepan over medium-high heat. When the pan is hot, add 1 tablespoon of butter along with the chicken. Cook until the chicken is done, then remove it from the pan and set it aside.

3. Lower the heat to low and add the remaining 5 tablespoons of butter to the pan along with the onions, carrots, celery, garlic, and thyme. Cook the veggies until tender, about 10 minutes. Then stir in the flour until no lumps remain. Stirring constantly, slowly add small amounts of the chicken stock to the pan, incorporating the liquid before adding more. When all the chicken stock has been added, add the half-and-half and bring the mixture to a boil. When the mixture has come to a boil, lower the heat and simmer, stirring frequently until the gravy/potpie filling has thickened, 10 minutes.

4. Season to taste with salt and black pepper, and add the peas.

5. Carefully lay 1 of the pie crusts into a 9 inch pie pan, and pour in the gravy/potpie filling. Next, lay the second crust over the top. Seal the edges together, and pinch to flute around the rim. Beat the egg in a small bowl, and brush some of it lightly over the top of the pie.

6. Bake until the pie crust is browned and the filling is bubbling, about 30 minutes.

7. Serve immediately, or cool and cover tightly to freeze and use within 1 month.

 **15** MIN — Prep Time

 **50** MIN — Cook Time

 **6-8** SERVINGS — Makes

3

5

5

# TEX-MEX FIESTA RICE

When Dave and I first were married, I would consistently make rice dishes. They were simple, quick, and made me feel like a domestic goddess. Also, rice is easily one of the most enjoyable foods on the planet. It's the most versatile, too! For your next fiesta, please enjoy this scrumptious dish. The best part? You can mix this recipe with any protein, like chicken or fish, and have yourself a full dinner.

# INGREDIENTS

1 tablespoon olive oil

1 cup diced onion

1 red bell pepper, diced

1 garlic clove, minced

1 tablespoon Fiesta Blend

1 teaspoon ground cumin

1 cup long-grain white rice

1 (14-ounce) can black beans, rinsed

1 (14-ounce) can chopped fire-roasted tomatoes

1 cup vegetable broth

½ teaspoon salt

1 cup frozen corn

1 cup grated Pepper Jack cheese

¼ cup chopped fresh cilantro

1 ripe avocado, cubed

1 cup chopped fresh tomatoes

# DIRECTIONS

1. Preheat a large (12- to 15-inch) ovenproof skillet over medium-high heat. When the pan is hot, add the oil, onion, and bell pepper to the pan.

2. Sauté until the onions and peppers are crisp-tender, 3 to 4 minutes. Then add the garlic, Fiesta Blend, cumin, and rice to the pan. Continue to cook, stirring to combine until the grains of rice are completely coated.

3. Then add the beans, fire-roasted tomatoes, broth, and salt to the pan. Stir to combine, cover the pan, and lower the heat to maintain a simmer.

4. Simmer until the rice is tender, and all the liquid is absorbed, about 20 to 25 minutes.

5. When the rice is done, preheat the oven to 400°F.

6. Add the corn to the pan, and mix to combine. Sprinkle with cheese, and bake until the cheese is bubbling.

7. Serve the rice immediately with the fresh cilantro, avocado, and chopped tomatoes.

8. For a make-ahead meal, freeze the finished rice in individual containers. To serve, thaw overnight in the refrigerator, and gently reheat.

 **15** MIN — *Prep Time*

 **25-30** MIN — *Cook Time*

 **4** SERVINGS — *Makes*

**NOTES:**

*You can also bake this in a casserole dish. Simply transfer it from the skillet after the liquids have been added. Bake tightly covered until the rice has absorbed all the liquid, then add the corn, sprinkle with cheese, and continue to bake until the cheese is bubbling. Freeze the casserole whole or portion into individual containers.*

# DADDY'S SPAGHETTI SAUCE

I often give my mom loads of shout-outs for her recipes, but the truth is, both of my parents are awesome cooks. Daddy has all kinds of good dishes, but his most famous creation is the spaghetti sauce he's spent years perfecting. He made me promise to tell you that you should feel free to add a dash of this or a little of that and test different variations until you find your favorite.

# INGREDIENTS

2 tablespoons dried oregano

2 tablespoons dried basil

1 tablespoon paprika

1 tablespoon dried parsley

1 teaspoon garlic powder

1 teaspoon onion powder

¼ teaspoon dried rosemary

¼ teaspoon dried sage

¼ teaspoon dried thyme

¼ teaspoon dried marjoram

2 pounds ground beef and Italian sausage, 50/50 mix

4 garlic cloves, minced

1 large onion, finely diced

1 red bell pepper, finely diced

2 stalks celery, finely diced

2 (12-ounce) cans diced tomatoes

1 (32-ounce box) beef broth

# DIRECTIONS

1. *Mix together all the dried spices and set them aside.*

2. *Place a large stockpot over medium-high heat. When the pan is hot, add the ground beef and Italian sausage. Brown the meat, breaking it up into small pieces with a spoon as you cook it.*

3. *When the meat is browned, add the minced garlic, diced onion, bell pepper, and celery. Cook just until the veggies begin to soften, 4 to 5 minutes. Then add the mixture of spices and cook, stirring for another minute before adding the diced tomatoes and beef broth.*

4. *Bring the sauce to a boil, then lower the heat to maintain a bare simmer. Simmer the sauce to blend the flavors, stirring occasionally, for about 1½ hours. Add additional liquid (beef broth) only if needed.*

5. *For the best flavor, let the sauce sit overnight in the refrigerator before serving.*

6. *This makes enough for 3 pounds of spaghetti, so you can also divide it into 3 freezer-safe containers and freeze for later use.*

 Prep Time 20 MIN

 Cook Time 2 HOURS

 Makes 12 SERVINGS

## NOTES:

*Fill a freezer bag with sauce and remove as much air as possible before sealing the bag. This helps prevent unwanted freezer burn. Lay the bag on a flat surface in the freezer. Alternatively, freeze the bags on a baking sheet tray to ensure the bags freeze flat. When freezing multiple bags, stack them to use minimal space. Freezing the bags flat not only utilizes valuable freezer space, but it also helps speed up freezing and thawing times. Be sure to label and date the bags. Frozen sauce keeps for 3 months. When you are ready to use the sauce, simply thaw, reheat, and toss with cooked pasta. In no time, you've got yourself a quick homemade meal!*

# RANCH BEEF STEW

I love anything with ranch in the title and I looooovveee me some beef stew. In this recipe, I figured we'd combine the two greatest things on earth and create the ultimate Ranch Beef Stew! This bad boy is perfect to serve on cozy winter nights or for a Sunday supper with some fresh sourdough bread and butter.

# INGREDIENTS

1 tablespoon olive oil

2 pounds beef stew meat, cut into 1-inch cubes

2 cups diced onion, ½-inch pieces

2 large carrots, peeled and sliced into ½-inch pieces (2 cups)

1 red bell pepper, cut into 1-inch cubes (2 cups)

1 pound Yukon Gold potatoes, cut into 2-inch pieces

3 cups beef broth

2 garlic cloves, minced

3 tablespoons Southwestern Ranch Seasoning

2 tablespoons tomato paste

1 tablespoon Worcestershire sauce

½ teaspoon black pepper

½ teaspoon salt

2 tablespoons cornstarch

¼ cup water

1½ cups frozen peas

1 cup frozen corn

¼ cup chopped cilantro

# DIRECTIONS

1. Preheat a large skillet over medium-high heat. When the pan is hot, add the olive oil and cubed stew meat. Brown the meat, 4 to 5 minutes, and remove it from the pan.

2. Place the stew meat in a 6-quart slow cooker along with the prepared onion, carrots, bell pepper, and potatoes.

3. Mix together the beef broth, garlic, Southwestern Ranch Seasoning, tomato paste, Worcestershire sauce, black pepper, and salt until smooth.

4. Pour the beef broth mixture over the meat and vegetables, and cook on low for 8 to 9 hours, or until the beef and vegetables are tender.

5. When the beef and vegetables are tender, mix the cornstarch together with ¼ cup water until no lumps remain. Stir the cornstarch mixture into the stew, along with the peas and corn. Cook on high until the cornstarch thickens, 15 to 30 minutes.

6. Mix in the cilantro and serve immediately. The leftovers freeze well.

7. To prepare this ahead for the freezer, mix together the peas and corn, and place them in a separate bag and freeze alongside the stew. Place the browned stew meat and remaining vegetables into a large gallon-size freezer-safe ziplock. Mix together the beef broth, garlic, Southwestern Ranch Seasoning, tomato paste, Worcestershire sauce, black pepper, and salt until smooth. Pour the beef broth mixture into the bag with the beef and vegetables. Carefully remove the air from the bag, and seal it before placing it in the freezer. To use, thaw the stew mixture overnight in the refrigerator before placing it in the slow cooker.

 **20** MIN *Prep Time*

 **8-9** HOURS *Cook Time*

 **8-10** SERVINGS *Makes*

# LEMON-PESTO CHICKEN

From the colors to the flavors, this dish is utterly vibrant! It's like your new favorite casserole, only . . . it's minus the noodles, rice, or potatoes that usually throw us off our diets. In this instance we're rocking some lean protein, seasonal veggies, and a sauce that's so good you may actually wet your pants. This is a must try for your make-ahead lineup.

# INGREDIENTS

1 boneless, skinless chicken breast, (about 6 oz) cut into 1-inch pieces

1 (10-ounce) package frozen whole green beans

½ cup prepared pesto

2 tablespoons freshly squeezed lemon juice

1 tablespoon cornstarch

½ teaspoon salt

¼ teaspoon black pepper

1 cup grated mozzarella cheese

# DIRECTIONS

1. Place the cubed chicken and frozen green beans into a 8 x 6 x 2-inch casserole dish.

2. In a mixing bowl, combine the pesto, lemon juice, cornstarch, salt, and black pepper until thoroughly mixed.

3. Pour the sauce over the chicken and green beans, and toss to coat everything evenly with the pesto sauce.

4. Bake the casserole right away, or cover tightly and freeze up to 1 month.

5. To bake the frozen casserole, first thaw it overnight in the refrigerator.

6. Then bake in an oven (preheated to 375°F) for 15 to 20 minutes or until the casserole is starting to bubble, stirring at the halfway point.

7. When the juices are starting to bubble around the edges, remove the casserole from the oven and top with grated mozzarella cheese.

8. Turn the heat up to 425°F and return the casserole to the oven. Bake until bubbling, and browned, and until the chicken is completely done. Serve immediately.

 **15 MIN** *Prep Time*

 **30 MIN** *Cook Time*

 **4 SERVINGS** *Makes*

# DINNER ON THE GRILL

A few years ago I tagged along with Dave on a work trip down to Argentina. My reason for excitement was multilayered. (1) I'd never been to South America before and it felt ultrafancy to go. (2) My big sister came to town and bravely watched our boys for a week so we could get some alone time. And (3) the Argentinian office of the company my husband works for is—and this *should not* be taken lightly—literally filled with the most beautiful bunch of humans you've ever seen in your whole life. They are fun and funny and kind and they drink more than anybody you've ever met while encouraging you to do the same . . . They are also so attractive it doesn't even seem possible. I mean, if I showed you a picture right now, you would have a visceral reaction to that gorgeous bunch—I know it's true because I saved a photo on my phone for a year afterward that I would randomly bring out at dinner parties to stun the crowd, but I digress.

We went to Buenos Aires, and it was pure magic. We rode on the front of a speedboat down a gigantic river I still don't know the name of. We had dinner at restaurants so hip we barely got inside. And on the very last day, those beautiful South Americans invited us over for a polo match followed by an *asado*. Now, just to clarify, we went to a polo match. In. Their. Backyard. Because in BA they have backyard polo matches, *with the horses they own*, the way we might have a pickup game of basketball or flag football on Thanksgiving. I have honest-to-blog photos of Dave and me riding some horses our friend owned like it was the most normal thing in the world.

Afterward, high on life, we went to someone's home for the *asado* portion of the day . . . which is a fancy term for cooking every kind of animal in a three-mile radius on a giant grill in the yard.

It was heaven.

We ate like it was our part-time job and drank malbec like the antidote was inside of every bottle, and somewhere along the way we forgot the cardinal rule of traveling to another country.

We drank the water.

Just to be clear—there's nothing wrong with most water in most countries you go to . . . it's only that our systems weren't used to the water there and, well, how can I put this delicately?

We prayed for death in a five-star Argentinian hotel that night.

We were violently ill.

Like, lose all sense of propriety or romance and pray that your partner scrubs the horror of what came afterward from his memory so that he'll still want to make out with you again someday.

The point (besides telling a horrifically unappetizing story as an intro to a cookbook chapter) is that I'd do it all again.

If you told me I could skip the illness, but it meant that I would also miss out on that incredible day when we got to have a cookout in Argentina, I wouldn't do it.

Some of the best memories I have in my whole life happened on a hot day, at a barbecue. It doesn't matter when it happens or where, there's always something magical about having everyone outside enjoying the weather and the company and feeling like life is pretty darn fantastic . . . even if you don't own polo ponies.

# CEDAR-PLANK SALMON

Confession: I used to hate salmon. I know it's a great source of omega-3, etc., but I didn't really grow up eating fish, and this particular one was always a bit too pungent for my tastes. That was until I had my first cedar-plank salmon. This preparation is out of this world! Since you marinate the fish in soy and ginger, it's got a great tang, and the cedar plank adds a great smoky flavor. Also, you're cooking on cedar, which makes your guests think you're a total grill master.

# INGREDIENTS

1 tablespoon olive oil

2 tablespoons Moroccan Seasoning

1 garlic clove, minced

3 tablespoons brown sugar

3 tablespoons freshly squeezed lemon juice

½ teaspoon salt

1 salmon fillet (3 pounds)

1 cedar plank (16 x 7 inch food-grade cedar), soaked in water for 4 hours

1 tablespoon chopped fresh cilantro

1 lemon, cut into wedges or slices for serving

# DIRECTIONS

1. Preheat a grill over medium heat until it reaches a steady temperature of 350° to 375°F.

2. While the grill heats, mix together the olive oil, Moroccan Seasoning, garlic, brown sugar, lemon juice, and salt until combined.

3. Rinse the salmon fillet, and pat it dry with paper towels.

4. Place the presoaked cedar plank on the grill to heat for 4 to 5 minutes. Then place the salmon fillet on the plank, and brush the marinade evenly over the top.

5. Grill the salmon until just barely done, this will take about 25 minutes for a fillet that's 1¾ inches at the thickest part.

6. When the salmon is cooked, sprinkle with the cilantro and serve immediately with lemon wedges.

 **10** MIN — *Prep Time*

 **20-25** MIN — *Cook Time*

 **8** SERVINGS — *Makes*

# FOIL-WRAP FISH BAKE

This dish is like having a big seafood boil . . . only without the mess! You take all the classic ingredients—seafood, red potatoes, and corn—then cover them in a holy trinity of butter, garlic, and dill and allow the grill to turn them into something magical. The best part? Dipping a piece of toasty sourdough bread in the butter and drippings.

# INGREDIENTS

1 pound red potatoes,
cut into ½-inch cubes

3 ears corn on the cob, shucked,
and cut into 2-inch slices

1 pound halibut fillet(s),
cut into 4 pieces

½ pound extra large shrimp

6 tablespoons salted butter, melted

1 garlic clove, minced

2 tablespoons snipped fresh dill

1 teaspoon black pepper

½ teaspoon salt

Serve with:
crusty sourdough bread
and lemon wedges

# DIRECTIONS

1. Preheat a grill over medium heat until it reaches a steady temperature between 350° and 400°F.

2. While the grill heats, prepare all the ingredients. Start by cutting 4 pieces of foil about 18 inches long each.

3. In the front half of each of the 4 sheets of foil, place one quarter of the potatoes and evenly divide the corn on the cob pieces.

4. Next place a halibut fillet on top of the potatoes on each foil sheet. Then add 4 shrimp around each halibut fillet.

5. Stir together the melted butter, garlic, dill, black pepper, and salt. Pour the mixture evenly over each of the four fish fillets.

6. Carefully fold the long end of foil over the top of the fish and vegetables. Double fold to seal the three edges on each of the foil packets.

7. Place the packets on the heated grill and cook until the fish and shrimp are cooked through, and the potatoes are done, 12 to 15 minutes.

8. Serve immediately with crusty sourdough bread and lemon wedges.

 15 MIN — Prep Time

 12-15 MIN — Cook Time

 4 SERVINGS — Makes

# GRILLED PIZZA PARTY

A couple of years ago I made a grilled pizza from scratch for a celebration, and the results were stellar. The one downside is that the process of making pizza dough is incredibly time-consuming. Don't get me wrong—the end results are delicious, but I personally don't have the time to spend hours kneading dough. In an attempt to simplify the process, I now use a premade dough, which works just as well as the from-scratch variety.

# INGREDIENTS

2 pounds store-bought pizza dough

1 can/jar pizza sauce
(I used ⅓ cup on 2 of the 4 pizzas)

## WHITE PIZZA SAUCE:

¼ cup olive oil

1 garlic clove, minced

1 teaspoon Zesty Italian seasoning

## TOPPINGS:

1 pound mozzarella cheese, grated (about 4 cups)

1 cup grated Parmesan cheese

1 package sliced pepperoni

1 cup cooked sausage (I used hot Italian sausage)

4 to 6 slices Canadian bacon

¼ to ½ cup black olives

1 cup thinly sliced red and green bell peppers

1 cup thinly sliced red onion

## OPTIONAL TOPPINGS:

tomatoes

pineapple

basil, cooked or raw sliced

mushrooms

crumbled feta cheese, and so on.

# DIRECTIONS

1. *Preheat the grill over medium heat. While the grill heats, assemble as many toppings as you'd like.*

2. *To make the White Pizza Sauce, mix together the olive oil, garlic, and Zesty Italian seasoning, and set it aside to let the flavors develop.*

3. *Cut the pizza dough into quarters. Pat out each of the four pieces of dough on a sheet of parchment paper until it's about 8 inches across.*

4. *Lightly brush the pizzas with your choice of white or red pizza sauce, then top with mozzarella and a sprinkling of Parmesan. Finally, top with the toppings of your choice.*

5. *Grill each pizza over medium heat, maintaining a temperature between 350° and 400°F for about 8 minutes, or until the dough is thoroughly cooked and the cheese is bubbling.*

6. *Serve immediately with any desired fresh toppings, like chopped tomatoes and basil.*

 **10-20** MIN *Prep Time*

 **6-8** MIN *Cook Time*

 **4-6** SERVINGS *Makes*

# GRILLED TURKEY BURGERS
## *with green apple and chutney*

I often find myself on a never-ending high-protein diet, so I'm constantly dreaming up new ways to approach the same old protein-laden dinners. I threw these turkey burgers together one night, and they were good enough to share . . . . Who says you can't put fruit into your patty?? Not me! I'm a fan of mixing and matching sweet and savory pairings of all kinds. I encourage you to try some not-so-common pairings whenever you're feeling adventurous. You never know what new go-to meal you are on the verge of creating.

## INGREDIENTS

1 package ground turkey
(1½ pounds)

½ cup grated green apple

⅓ cup mango ginger chutney

2 teaspoons Moroccan Seasoning

1 teaspoon salt

1 teaspoon black pepper

1 garlic clove, minced

Cooking spray

4 hamburger buns

## TOPPINGS:

½ small red onion, slivered

1 cup thinly sliced cucumber

½ cup roughly chopped cilantro

¼ cup Greek yogurt

## DIRECTIONS

1. Preheat a grill over medium heat until it reaches a steady temperature between 350° and 400°F.

2. While the grill heats, mix together the turkey, apple, chutney, Moroccan Seasoning, salt, black pepper, and garlic until thoroughly combined. Form the mixture into 4 patties.

3. Clean the grill and spray it well with cooking spray/oil. Place the patties on the grill and grill until just done in the middle, 8 to 10 minutes per side.

4. While the burgers are grilling, prepare the toppings.

5. If desired, toast the buns on the grill during the last few minutes of grilling time.

6. Serve the burgers with the buns and toppings.

 **15** MIN *Prep Time*

 **15–20** MIN *Cook Time*

**4** SERVINGS *Makes*

# SHRIMP KABOBS

Looking for some party-friendly nibbles that are sure to impress from the Fourth of July through Labor Day weekend? Look no further than grilled Shrimp Kabobs. They're full of flavor but require a minimal amount of cooking. We served up these yummy kabobs last summer to all of our friends, and they still ask for the recipe to this day. So here it is, guys! Enjoy!

# INGREDIENTS

1 pound large shrimp, fresh or thawed and drained

2 zucchini, sliced into ½-inch circles

2 cups cherry tomatoes

1 red onion, cut into 1-inch pieces

2 teaspoons Zesty Italian seasoning

¼ cup olive oil

2 tablespoons white wine vinegar

1 garlic clove (minced)

½ teaspoon salt

1 lemon, halved and sliced into ¼-inch pieces

Cooking spray

# DIRECTIONS

1. *If you're using wooden skewers, be sure to soak them in water for at least 2 hours before grilling.*

2. *Place the shrimp, zucchini, cherry tomatoes, and red onions into a large mixing bowl.*

3. *In a small bowl, combine the Zesty Italian seasoning, olive oil, vinegar, garlic, and salt together until mixed.*

4. *Pour the marinade over the shrimp and veggies and toss to combine.*

5. *Thread the shrimp and vegetables onto the skewers, alternating as you go until all the shrimp and vegetables have been used, about 12 to 15 skewers. Place a lemon slice on each end of the skewers.*

6. *Preheat a grill over medium-high heat until it reaches a steady temperature between 400° and 450°F.*

7. *Clean the grill and spray it with cooking spray/oil, and then place the shrimp skewers evenly over the surface of the grill.*

8. *Cook for 5 to 7 minutes per side, or until the shrimp is done and the vegetables are crisp-tender. Serve immediately.*

**20** MIN — *Prep Time*

**10-15** MIN — *Cook Time*

**4** SERVINGS — *Makes*

# TERIYAKI CHICKEN KABOBS

Once in a while, I'll get to tag along with Dave on a work trip (I usually end up picking the trip that puts me in a tropical location). While Dave spends his time in meetings and speaking at conferences, I spend my time eating massive breakfasts, walking around and getting to know the city, and taking long, long naps. It is, without question, the most relaxing getaway! In honor of island living, fire up these sweet yet savory Teriyaki Chicken Kabobs.

# INGREDIENTS

1 package boneless, skinless chicken thighs (1½ pounds, or 4 thighs)

1 red bell pepper, cut into 1-inch cubes

1 green bell pepper, cut into 1-inch cubes

½ cup sliced scallions, the white and light green parts

3 cups fresh pineapple chunks

Cooking spray

## TERIYAKI SAUCE:

2 garlic cloves, minced

2 teaspoons minced ginger

½ cup soy sauce

½ cup brown sugar

2 tablespoons rice wine vinegar

2 tablespoons mirin (optional)

# DIRECTIONS

1. If you're using wooden skewers, be sure to soak them in water for at least 2 hours before grilling.

2. Make the teriyaki sauce by combining all the sauce ingredients in a medium-size saucepan (including the mirin, if using). Bring the mixture to a boil, then reduce the heat and simmer until reduced and slightly thickened, about 20 minutes. It will yield about ¾ cup.

3. While the sauce simmers, prepare the chicken, vegetables, and pineapple. Thread the chicken, vegetables, and pineapple onto the skewers, alternating as you go, until all the ingredients have been used. There will be around 15 skewers.

4. Preheat a grill over medium heat until you reach a steady temperature between 350° and 400°F.

5. When the sauce is finished, brush about ½ cup over the surface of the skewers, reserving the remaining ¼ cup sauce.

6. Clean the grill and spray it well with cooking spray/oil. Place the skewers evenly over the surface of the grill.

7. Cook for 8 to 10 minutes per side, or until the chicken is done and the skewers are browned and caramelized.

8. Serve the skewers immediately, with the reserved sauce if desired.

**20** MIN — *Prep Time*

**40** MIN — *Cook Time*

**4** SERVINGS — *Makes*

# MARINATED FLANK STEAK

The secret to the best flank steak? The best marinade!! Massage the marinade into the steak and then place it in the fridge for at least an hour. I'll tell you what, guys, I think any good marinade is better if you let it hang out overnight. But that's just my opinion. You do you!

## INGREDIENTS

1 flank steak (1 ½ pounds)

¼ cup soy sauce

1 tablespoon minced ginger

2 garlic cloves, minced

¼ cup thinly sliced scallions, the white part

2 tablespoons thinly sliced scallions, the green part

¼ cup honey, or brown sugar

1 teaspoon toasted sesame oil

Cooking spray

### GARNISH:

1 to 2 tablespoons thinly sliced scallions, the green part

## DIRECTIONS

1. Place the steak in a large gallon-size ziplock.

2. Mix together the soy sauce, ginger, garlic, scallions, honey (or brown sugar), and sesame oil.

3. Pour the marinade in over the flank steak and carefully remove the air from the bag while sealing it.

4. Refrigerate and marinate for at least 2 hours or overnight.

5. Preheat the grill over medium-high heat until it reaches a temperature between 400° and 450°F.

6. Clean the grill and spray it with cooking spray/oil. Place the steak on the grill and grill for 6 to 8 minutes per side for medium doneness.

7. Let the steak rest on a cutting board for 5 to 10 minutes before thinly slicing it against the grain.

8. Serve with the remaining scallions sprinkled over the top.

 **2** HOURS — Prep Time

 **15** MIN — Cook Time

 **4-6** SERVINGS — Makes

# GRILLED PORK SATAY

Want to give your guests the entire rainbow of protein options to choose from? We've got chicken! Check! Salmon? Check! Steak? Check! Tofu? Throw your guests a protein curveball by serving up some grilled pork satay to add variety to your barbecue. The sauce is the key ingredient that really brings out the best parts of this tasty recipe. It will be the best satay that they never saw coming.

# INGREDIENTS

1 pork tenderloin (2 pounds)        ¼ cup soy sauce        Cooking spray

## SATAY SAUCE:

1 cup coconut milk        ¼ cup peanut butter        1 garlic clove, minced        1 teaspoon Moroccan Seasoning

¼ cup soy sauce        ¼ cup brown sugar        1 tablespoon minced ginger        ½ cup thinly sliced scallions

## GARNISH:

2 tablespoons thinly sliced scallions        1 tablespoon chopped cilantro        1 lime, cut into wedges

# DIRECTIONS

1. If you're using wooden skewers, be sure to soak them in water for at least 2 hours before grilling.

2. Make the Satay Sauce by placing all the sauce ingredients into a saucepan. Bring the mixture to a boil, then reduce the heat to low. Simmer until the sauce is slightly thickened, about 10 minutes. There will be around 1½ cups sauce.

3. While the sauce is cooking, prepare the pork by cutting it into strips 1 by ½ inch thick and 6 to 8 inches long.

4. Place the pork strips into a gallon-size ziplock bag and add ½ cup of the Satay Sauce with ¼ cup soy sauce. Carefully remove the air from the bag and seal it.

5. Marinate the pork in the refrigerator for at least 2 hours or overnight.

6. When you're ready to grill, preheat the grill at medium-high heat until it reaches a steady temperature between 400° and 450°F.

7. While the grill heats, thread the marinated pork onto the skewers; there will be around 20.

8. Clean the grill and spray it well with cooking spray/oil. Place the skewers evenly over the surface of the grill and lower the heat to medium.

9. Cook for 8 to 10 minutes per side, or until the pork is cooked through.

10. Serve the pork satay with the reserved 1 cup of satay sauce, scallions, cilantro, and lime wedges.

**4 HOURS** Prep Time

**25-30 MIN** Cook Time

**8 SERVINGS** Makes

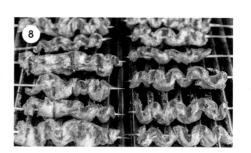

# GRILLED MUSHROOM KABOBS
## *with Balsamic Marinade*

Holler out to all my vegetarians! I haven't forgotten all of my veggie lovers out there (myself included). Just because you're not eating meat doesn't mean you have to miss out on all of the summer fun at the grill. Chow down on these delicious grilled mushroom kabobs—just writing about them makes my mouth water. YUM!

# INGREDIENTS

1½ pounds cremini mushrooms, cleaned

1 red onion, cut into 1-inch cubes

Cooking spray

## MARINADE:

¼ cup balsamic vinegar

1 tablespoon honey mustard

2 tablespoons olive oil

½ teaspoon salt

¼ teaspoon black pepper

1 teaspoon Zesty Italian seasoning

## GARNISH:

1 tablespoon chopped basil

Reduced balsamic vinegar for drizzling

# DIRECTIONS

1. *If you're using wooden skewers, be sure and soak them in water for at least 2 hours before grilling.*

2. *Whisk together all the ingredients for the marinade until completely emulsified.*

3. *Place the mushrooms and onion in a medium-size mixing bowl. Pour the marinade over the top and toss to combine.*

4. *Preheat the grill over medium heat until it maintains a temperature between 350° and 400°F.*

5. *Thread the mushrooms and onions onto the skewers, alternating between the two. You will have around 12 skewers.*

6. *Clean the grill and spray it with cooking spray/oil. Place the skewers evenly over the surface of the grill and grill for 5 to 7 minutes per side, or until the mushrooms are tender and browned.*

7. *Serve the mushroom kabobs with the chopped basil and reduced balsamic drizzled over the top.*

 **15** MIN *Prep Time*

 **10-15** MIN *Cook Time*

 **4** SERVINGS *Makes*

# GRILLED-CORN TOSTADAS
## *with Hummus*

Let's face it, grilling and cookouts are a blast to host in the summer, but we also want to balance chowing down with keeping our summer bods in relatively good shape. I've got the perfect healthy summer salad that you can customize to fit the bill. Sure, it's on a tostada shell (baby steps), but you can totally eat this by itself or as a topping on grilled chicken or fish. I'm pairing this recipe with hummus to add some protein without adding meat. Rock it your way, and rock that swimsuit, girl.

# INGREDIENTS

- 4 ears corn on the cob, shucked
- 1 small red onion, diced
- ½ cup red wine vinegar
- 1 can black beans

- 2 Roma tomatoes, diced
- 1 red bell pepper, diced
- 2 avocados, diced
- 1 teaspoon garlic powder

- 1 teaspoon paprika
- ½ teaspoon cumin
- ½ teaspoon salt
- ½ teaspoon black pepper

- Tostada shells for serving
- ½ cup crumbled cotija cheese
- ¼ cup fresh cilantro
- 1 container of your fave flavor of hummus

# DIRECTIONS

1. *Grill the corn on a stovetop or outdoor grill until charred all around. You can also cook it under a broiler until charred. Allow to cool.*

2. *Combine the chopped red onion and red wine vinegar in a small bowl. Allow to sit for at least 30 minutes.*

3. *Cut the corn kernels off the cob and throw them into a large bowl. Toss in the black beans, tomatoes, red bell pepper, avocado, and seasonings. Add the onions with only some of the red wine vinegar. Not all of it. Toss to combine. Taste and adjust seasonings (or red wine vinegar) accordingly.*

4. *Serve on top of store-bought tostada shells. Sprinkle with crumbled cotija cheese and fresh cilantro. Enjoy!*

**15 MIN** *Prep Time*

**15 MIN** *Cook Time*

**6 SERVINGS** *Makes*

# SOUP FOR DINNER

My name is Rachel, and I'm a soup lover.

I love any kind of soup, at any time of year, even in the middle of sweltering July with the exception of *one* thing . . . I hate cold soup. I don't understand it. Why would you take a perfectly delicious, belly-warming dish like soup and serve it cold? What kind of monster does that? A couple of years ago we were on a date at a fancy new restaurant and they had a seasonal corn soup on the menu. Corn soup is my ultimate soup-crush, so I was laser-focused on that menu item. When I read that it came with a "homemade corn-nut garnish," I was near euphoric. Basically, it was like fancy restaurant soup mixed with homemade junk food . . . how could I not get it? Then it came and it was beautiful and I took that giant soup spoon (the one you could also use for planting perennial blooms)

and I took a big ole bite of that thing. It was cold. My taste buds still shudder in remembrance. I called over our waiter (though I would sooner die than complain at a restaurant) and politely told him that the soup was a bit cold and could I please get another because the flavor was awesome.

"Oh, that's a summer soup," he told me. "It's to be served chilled."

On this point we will have to agree to disagree. All soup: summer soup, winter soup, stews, purees—you name it—should be hot in my personal opinion, and since this is my cookbook, you will find a wide array of absolutely delicious soups to enjoy and all of them are served hot, as God intended!

# SLOW COOKER LOADED BAKED POTATO SOUP

Back before I understood how calories worked—oh, say, fifteen years and twenty-five pounds ago—I adored loaded baked potato *anything*. A dip, an actual potato, or the creamy decadent soup you can choose as your "starter" at places like Outback or Chili's were my jam. Sadly, with age came the sad truth about exactly how many hours it would take me on a treadmill to work off a single bite. We're using the potatoes as a thickener so we use less cream, which means you can eat this without hating yourself.

# INGREDIENTS

5 slices bacon, cut into 1-inch pieces

3 garlic cloves, minced

1 large onion, minced

1 teaspoon fresh thyme, or
½ teaspoon dried thyme

2 tablespoons all-purpose flour

5 cups low-sodium chicken broth

3 pounds russet potatoes, peeled,
cut into ½-inch chunks

¼ cup whole milk

½ cup heavy cream

1½ cups sharp Cheddar cheese,
shredded

1½ teaspoon kosher salt

½ teaspoon black pepper

crumbled bacon

scallions, for serving

additional sharp Cheddar cheese,
shredded, for serving

sour cream, for serving

# DIRECTIONS

1. *In a large skillet, cook bacon over medium heat until crisp. Transfer cooked bacon to paper towel–lined plate and set aside. Keep 3 tablespoons of bacon fat and discard rest. You'll want to keep all those burned little bits in the pan. They will provide the onions with a lot of flavor.*

2. *Heat skillet with 3 tablespoons of bacon fat over medium heat. Add minced garlic and cook for 15 to 20 seconds, until fragrant. Add onions and thyme. Cook until onions have softened.*

3. *Add flour and stir to combine. Cook for about 1 minute and then slowly add 1 cup of chicken broth. Stir to combine. Transfer onion mixture (including all the browned bacon bits from pan) into slow cooker pot.*

4. *Add cut potatoes into slow cooker, followed by remaining 4 cups of chicken broth. Cover slow cooker with lid and set to cook for 4 to 5 hours on low.*

5. *Keep slow cooker on "keep warm" setting. Once potatoes are soft and tender, scoop out 3 cups of potato from slow cooker. Place in a large bowl and mash using a fork (spoon or muddler work, too). Add milk and cream. Stir to combine. Return mixture to slow cooker.*

6. *Add shredded cheese to slow cooker and stir to distribute. Cover slow cooker and let sit for 5 minutes, until cheese has melted. Season with 1½ teaspoon salt and ½ teaspoon black pepper. Sample and season according to taste. Serve with crumbled bacon, scallions, additional Cheddar cheese, sour cream, and other toppings you enjoy with baked potato.*

 **20** MIN *Prep Time*

 **4–5** HOURS *Cook Time*

 **4–6** SERVINGS *Makes*

# SLOW-COOKER WHITE BEAN SOUP

This is such a perfect recipe for a hearty dinner. The rich depth of flavor from the sausage pairs perfectly against the kale. Also, it's kale, which is super trendy with hipsters everywhere so this soup is actually cooler than you are. Well played.

# INGREDIENTS

1 tablespoon olive oil

1 pound ground sausage

1 yellow onion, diced

2 garlic cloves

4 cups chopped kale

1 teaspoon salt

1 teaspoon black pepper

2 (14-ounce) cans white beans, rinsed

6 cups chicken stock

¼ cup Parmesan cheese, for garnish

# DIRECTIONS

1. *Heat a large skillet over medium-high heat. Add the olive oil, and cook the sausage, crumbling with a wooden spoon, until brown and crispy. Stir in the onions and garlic and cook until soft. Add the kale, a handful at a time and sauté until wilted.*

2. *Transfer the sausage and kale mixture to a slow-cooker, and add in the salt, pepper, white beans and chicken stock.*

*Cover and cook on high for 3 hours or on low for 6 hours.*

3. *Serve with a sprinkling of Parmesan cheese. Enjoy!*

 **10** MIN — *Prep Time*

 **3** HOURS — *Cook Time*

 **8** SERVINGS — *Makes*

# TURKEY AND WILD RICE SOUP

One of my passions—besides Beyoncé and wishing that bangs would work with my face shape—is creating delicious recipes using leftovers. For this book, I wanted to make sure that we created another cool leftover recipe for y'all, and boy have we ever! This Turkey and Wild Rice Soup is the perfect way to use up leftover turkey or chicken. It's so delicious, and you can make it in your slow cooker so you won't have to battle the stove two days in a row.

# INGREDIENTS

1 yellow onion, diced

2 medium carrots, diced

2 celery stalks, diced

1 cup frozen peas

1 ½ cups wild rice blend

2 cups shredded leftover turkey or chicken

8 cups chicken stock

1 ½ teaspoons salt

1 teaspoon black pepper

3 tablespoons salted butter

3 tablespoons flour

1 ½ cups milk

# DIRECTIONS

1. *In your slow cooker, combine the onion, carrots, celery, peas, rice, turkey, stock, salt, and black pepper. Cook on high for 3 to 4 hours or on low for 6 to 8 hours, until rice is tender and soft.*

2. *Once rice is done, melt the butter in a medium saucepan with the flour. Cook for a few seconds and then whisk in the milk. Season with a bit of salt and black pepper. Cook until thickened and then stir into the soup. Cook for another 20 to 30 minutes until soup has thickened.*

3. *Serve with bread or crackers.*

**15** MIN — *Prep Time*

**4** HOURS — *Cook Time*

**8** SERVINGS — *Makes*

# BLACK BEAN SOUP

Slow Cooker Black Bean Soup, sounds complicated, right? Well no, it's not! You can totally make it happen . . . . I believe in you! Also, it's a surprisingly uncomplicated recipe. Just throw a couple of cans of black beans, some stock, spices, and sautéed veggies into a slow cooker, set, and forget. Turn it on when you head out to work, let it cook all day, and then come home to a delicious-smelling house and an even better tasting dinner!

## INGREDIENTS

1 tablespoon olive oil

1 yellow onion, diced

3 garlic cloves, minced

1 red bell pepper, diced

1 green bell pepper, diced

1 small jalapeño, minced (optional)

5 (15-ounce) cans black beans (drain 3 of the cans, and reserve the liquid of 2 cans)

4 cups vegetable or chicken stock

1 teaspoon salt

2 teaspoons black pepper

1 teaspoon paprika

1 teaspoon garlic powder

½ teaspoon ground cumin

### OPTIONAL TOPPINGS:

Sour cream, tortilla strips, diced tomato, green onion

## DIRECTIONS

1. Heat a large skillet over medium-high heat. Add the oil, and sauté the onion, garlic, and red and green peppers until tender, about 10 minutes. If using the optional jalapeño, add at this time.

2. In the slow cooker, combine the beans, sautéed veggies, stock, and seasonings. Cover and cook on low for about 6 hours or on high for 3 hours. About an hour before it's ready, you can smash some of the beans to help thicken the soup. Serve with any or all of the toppings listed. Enjoy!

 **25** MIN *Prep Time*

 **6** HOURS *Cook Time*

**6** SERVINGS *Makes*

# LENTIL SOUP
## with Bacon and Swiss Chard

You know that time of year when Starbucks cups switch to fall leaf–covered art, the air feels crisp, and the world smells like pumpkin spice? That means it's time for soups, scarves, and sweaters! When this delightful season is upon us, the first soup recipe I turn to is one that my mom used to make when I was younger . . . lentil soup. Though delicious, hers never tasted anywhere near as good as this yummy slow cooker lentil soup (no disrespect to my mama). This recipe has bacon and Swiss chard, carrots, and celery, too. It's an awesome recipe for fall and a great meal that you can eat all week long.

# INGREDIENTS

6 strips of bacon, chopped

1 medium yellow onion, chopped

2 large carrots, peeled and diced

3 stalks of celery, diced

2 garlic cloves, minced

4 cups loosely packed Swiss or red chard, stemmed and chopped

1 cup green lentils, rinsed

8 cups chicken broth or stock

1 (15-ounce) can diced tomatoes

1 bay leaf

1 teaspoon salt

¾ teaspoon black pepper

# DIRECTIONS

1. Set a skillet over medium-high heat with the bacon. Cook until crispy, about 8 minutes. Transfer the bacon, with a slotted spoon, to your slow cooker.

2. Add in the remaining ingredients, stirring to fully combine. Cover and cook on low for about 6 to 8 hours or on high for 3 to 4 hours, or until the lentils have softened. Taste before serving and adjust seasonings accordingly, adding more salt or black pepper as needed.

 *Prep Time* 20 MIN

 *Cook Time* 8 HOURS

 *Makes* 12 SERVINGS

# GREEN CHICKEN CHILI

Call me crazy, but I happen to love hot soup on a hot day. I know that sounds a little odd, but for some reason, I dig the strange combo. Then I started to write about my hot-on-hot addiction on social media and found out that I'm not alone in my cravings. My readers reached out, and it turns out they rave about the combo, too! So in honor of our shared love of hot soups during a hot summer, I came up with a new take on a classic chili . . . white bean chicken chili. It's perfect for hot summer days (and cold ones, too)!

# INGREDIENTS

2 pounds boneless, skinless chicken breasts, (about 1 pound) diced

2 pounds tomatillos, husked and rinsed

4 to 6 Anaheim chile peppers, seeded and diced

1 jalapeño, seeded and minced

1 large yellow onion, diced

3 garlic cloves, diced

3 cups chicken stock

2 teaspoons salt

2 teaspoons black pepper

1 teaspoon cumin

1 teaspoon dried oregano

1 lime, juiced

## TOPPINGS

sour cream

cheese

cilantro

tortillas (for serving)

# DIRECTIONS

1. *Combine all of the ingredients in a slow cooker (except the toppings, of course). And cook on low for 6 to 8 hours or on high for 2 to 4 hours. Right before serving, take the back of a spoon or a potato masher and break down the chicken into smaller pieces. Garnish with desired toppings and enjoy.*

**15** MIN *Prep Time*

**8** HOURS *Cook Time*

**6** SERVINGS *Makes*

# CORN CHOWDER

Years ago when we were in Hawaii, I tried coconut corn chowder at a local restaurant. Now, I should perhaps back up and tell you that corn chowder is one of my favorite foods on earth. I don't care where I am or what the restaurant specializes in, if I see it on the menu, I'm ordering it! But at this particular restaurant, the recipe was the most unique flavor combo I've ever had. Lime juice, jalapeño, coconut, lemon grass— it was totally unexpected and absolutely delicious! I loved it so much I had to figure out how to recreate it.

# INGREDIENTS

1 tablespoon coconut oil

1 large yellow onion, diced

2 garlic cloves, minced

1 jalapeño, seeded and chopped

2 (10-ounce) bags frozen corn, thawed, reserve ½ cup

1 (13.6-ounce) can full-fat coconut milk

3 cups water (or vegetable stock)

1½ teaspoons salt

½ teaspoon black pepper

1 tablespoon cornstarch

2 limes, juiced

½ cup fresh cilantro leaves

## TOPPINGS

2 Roma tomatoes, diced

¼ cup shredded coconut, large pieces

# DIRECTIONS

1. Set a large pot over medium-high heat with the coconut oil. Once melted, add in the onions and garlic and cook until soft and translucent, about 5 minutes. Stir in the jalapeño and corn (reserving about ½ cup of kernels) and cook for another 2 to 3 minutes.

2. Add the coconut milk and water and bring to a simmer. Season with a bit of salt and black pepper and cook uncovered for about 8 minutes. Mix a tablespoon of water with the cornstarch and then stir into the soup. Cook until thickened, about 5 minutes. Stir in the lime juice and cilantro. Adjust seasonings accordingly, adding more salt or black pepper as needed. Serve in bowls, and top each with the reserved corn, diced tomato, and coconut.

 **10 MIN** *Prep Time*

 **35 MIN** *Cook Time*

**4 SERVINGS** *Makes*

# SPICY BEEF ENCHILADA SOUP

This slow cooker Spicy Beef Enchilada Soup was born of necessity . . . meaning I needed to figure out dinner—and quickly. I looked in the freezer and found a package of cooked ground beef I keep around for just such an occasion. In the pantry I had a big can of red enchilada sauce, and the rest is history. Both Dave and I were shocked with how tasty this is for a thrown-together soup. I know a lot of you are big fans of the green chicken enchilada soup from my last cookbook. . . . Well, this option is a good way to change up the flavor and utilize a lot of your pantry staples.

# INGREDIENTS

2 pounds cooked ground beef

1 (28-ounce) can red enchilada sauce

1 (14-ounce) can pinto beans, drained and rinsed

1 (28-ounce) can diced tomatoes

2 cups water

1 (4-ounce) can green peppers

1 teaspoon garlic powder

1 teaspoon black pepper

1 (14-ounce) can corn, or 1 (10-ounce) bag frozen corn

6 corn tortillas, cut into 1" pieces

Serve with: Grated cheddar cheese, sour cream, black olives, diced tomatoes, or pico de gallo, chopped cilantro

# DIRECTIONS

1. Place the cooked ground beef, enchilada sauce, pinto beans, tomatoes, water, green peppers, garlic powder, and black pepper into a 6-quart slow cooker.

2. Cover and cook for 7-8 hours on low. About 15 minutes before the end of the cooking time, add the corn and stir to combine. Layer the corn tortilla pieces over the top of the soup, but do not stir them in. Cover and cook the remaining 15 minutes or until the tortillas have softened.

3. Serve with any desired toppings.

**NOTES:**

You can substitute turkey meat for ground beef if you like. I used medium red enchilada sauce and it was pretty spicy, so choose with caution.

 **20** MIN  *Prep Time*

 **8** HOURS  *Cook Time*

 **6-8** SERVINGS  *Makes*

# TORTELLINI MINESTRONE

This Tortellini Minestrone is my go-to classic. This soup is to me what "The Way You Look Tonight" is to Sinatra; it never gets old and always goes down smooth. I've been making it for years now, and I'm excited to give it the spotlight it deserves. I make it all year-round, but it's the perfect soup to make in the winter because you get the heartiness from the minestrone with the flavor of the tortellini. And, since we're using store-bought tortellini, it's super easy to pull off!

# INGREDIENTS

1 tablespoon olive oil

1 yellow onion, diced

2 garlic cloves, chopped

4 large celery stalks, diced

2 large carrots, peeled and diced

2 (14-ounce) cans diced tomatoes with juice

2 (14-ounce) cans kidney beans, rinsed and drained

1 teaspoon salt

½ teaspoon black pepper

2 teaspoons dried oregano

2 teaspoons dried basil

4 cups chicken stock

1 (9-ounce) package store-bought cheese tortellini

grated Parmesan cheese, for serving

# DIRECTIONS

**1.** *Set a large pot over medium-high heat with the olive oil. Once hot, add in the onions and garlic and cook until soft and translucent, about 5 minutes. Stir in the celery and carrots and cook for about 3 to 5 minutes longer. Stir in the diced tomatoes with their juice and the beans. Season with salt, black pepper, oregano, and basil.*

**2.** *Add the chicken stock and bring to a simmer. Cook until the veggies soften, about 10 to 15 minutes. Add the tortellini and cook until they float, about 3 to 5 minutes. Serve the soup with a sprinkling of cheese on top.*

 **15** MIN *Prep Time*

 **25** MIN *Cook Time*

 **8** SERVINGS *Makes*

# CREAMY BASIL TOMATO

When I was a little girl, my Grandma Neeley made us soup almost every day for lunch. The options were always: cream of chicken or tomato . . . Both of them were from Campbell's. She never, ever left them as is, though. Grandma was the OG when it came to doctoring up food from a can. I like to think of this creamy basil tomato soup as the grown-up version of what I ate when I was little. Grandma would approve.

# INGREDIENTS

1 tablespoon olive oil

½ yellow onion, finely diced

1 garlic clove, minced

2 (28-ounce) cans diced tomatoes

1 cup chicken stock, or vegetable stock for vegetarian

1 teaspoon black pepper

2 tablespoons brown sugar

½ cup heavy cream

1 teaspoon salt (this will vary depending on stock used)

## GARNISH:

¼ cup chopped fresh basil, plus extra for garnish

¼ cup grated Parmesan cheese

# DIRECTIONS

1. Heat a large stockpot over medium-high heat. When the pan is hot, add the olive oil, onions, and garlic. Sauté over medium heat until the onions are translucent, about 10 minutes.

2. Add the diced tomatoes, black pepper, and chicken/vegetable stock to the pan. Bring the soup to a boil, then reduce the heat to maintain a simmer. Simmer the soup, stirring occasionally until it thickens, about 25 minutes.

3. Strain the soup with a sieve, or carefully add the soup to a blender and blend until smooth. Return the soup to the pan, and add the brown sugar and heavy cream. Simmer for another 5 minutes, and season to taste with salt.

4. Stir in the basil and serve immediately, or serve the basil along with the grated Parmesan.

 **15** MIN *Prep Time*

 **45** MIN *Cook Time*

**4-6** SERVINGS *Makes*

# SALAD FOR DINNER

When I was a little girl, the fanciest restaurant in the whole wide world was Sizzler.

I'm not talking, *this is the nice place we go on a Thursday night*. I'm talking, we've got to be celebrating the Queen's birthday or something to be able to afford a trip to the all-you-can-eat buffet at Sizzler. It was a rare occurrence, and that salad bar buffet was the best thing I could possibly imagine for my life.

Sometimes Mema and Papa took us there after church. Sometimes the whole family might go for something really special. Once upon a time, my big sister Melody and I spent two weeks planning and producing a yard sale, and our entire profit went into a dinner at Sizzler. We got extra fro-yo and both agreed it was money well spent. I think the specialness of my Sizzler experience is what really solidified my love for gigantic salads. I would begin with a pile of lettuce and end with a plate so loaded with sundries it was a small miracle I made it back to my table without it exploding like Vesuvius.

I love a giant salad. I love using up thirty-three different leftovers to create one. I love a salad that skates a thin line between actual nutritional properties and really just a pile of junk covered with dressing. So in this chapter I've worked hard to come up with recipes that are full of great ingredients but big enough to keep you full all the way until breakfast tomorrow, no sneeze guard included.

# LAYERED COBB SALAD

During the summer months we have this Cobb salad for dinner at least once a week. I dig that the layers mean my kids can pick around anything they don't like, but we're still getting greens and protein in one serving. It's a great recipe to prep in advance and take for lunch throughout the week. I'd just suggest storing each ingredient separately until you're ready to eat it so it doesn't get soggy.

# INGREDIENTS

12 cups chopped romaine, from 1 large head

4 hard-boiled eggs, cubed

1½ cups cubed ham

1½ cups grated Cheddar cheese

2 cups chopped tomatoes

1 ripe avocado, cubed

½ cup cooked and crumbled bacon

½ cup minced red onion

## GREEK YOGURT RANCH DRESSING:

1 cup Greek yogurt

½ cup buttermilk

1½ teaspoons Southwestern Ranch seasoning

1 teaspoon salt

¼ teaspoon black pepper

# DIRECTIONS

1. *Mix together all the ingredients for the ranch dressing, and set it aside to let the flavors develop.*

2. *Place the chopped romaine into a large serving bowl.*

3. *Arrange the eggs, ham, cheese, tomatoes, avocado, bacon, and onion over the top of the lettuce.*

4. *Toss the salad with the desired amount of dressing, or serve the salad and dressing separately.*

 **30 MIN** *Prep Time*

 **4 SERVINGS** *Makes*

## HARD-BOILED EGGS

1. *Place the desired number of eggs into a saucepan and fill with cold water to 1 inch over the top of the eggs.*

2. *Bring the eggs to a boil, then remove the pan from the heat, cover, and let the eggs set up for 10 minutes.*

3. *Then place the eggs into an ice bath to cool for 15 minutes before peeling them.*

1

3

# COWBOY STEAK SALAD

This is a "salad" for people who only love meat and potatoes . . . or really, it's an excuse to eat steak and potatoes but still feel relatively good about yourself because you can tell people "Who me? I ate a salad for dinner." It really does fill me up as a complete dinner, but it's also a great option to bring to potlucks or get-togethers.

## INGREDIENTS

4 medium-size Yukon Gold potatoes (1 pound), cut into bite-size pieces

1 tablespoon olive oil

1 cup frozen corn

1 pound steak (1 to 2 pieces, depending on size; I used a sirloin)

6 cups mixed baby greens

1 small red onion, thinly sliced

2 cups chopped tomatoes

¼ cup blue cheese crumbles

### CREAMY JALAPEÑO RANCH VINAIGRETTE:

¼ cup white wine vinegar

2 teaspoons Southwestern Ranch seasoning

1 tablespoon minced jalapeño

1 garlic clove, minced

¼ cup buttermilk

¼ cup olive oil

1 teaspoon salt, or to taste

¼ cup blue cheese crumbles

## DIRECTIONS

1. Whisk together all the ingredients for the ranch vinaigrette, and set the dressing aside.

2. Preheat the oven to 400°F, and line a baking sheet with parchment paper. Spread the potatoes evenly on the baking sheet, and drizzle with olive oil. Roast the potatoes until tender, about 20 minutes. When the potatoes are done, turn off the oven, add the corn to the baking sheet with the potatoes, and let it cook in the residual oven heat for 5 minutes

3. While the potatoes are cooking, grill the steak over medium-high heat, turning at the halfway point. Cook until the desired doneness is reached, about 6 to 8 minutes per side for medium to well-done. Set the steak aside to cool while you assemble the salad.

4. Place the mixed greens into a large serving bowl, along with the red onions, tomatoes, and blue cheese. Top the salad with the warm roasted potato and corn mixture. Thinly slice the steak and add it to the salad bowl.

5. Drizzle with the dressing, or serve it on the side with the salad.

 **30** MIN *Prep Time*

 **20** MIN *Cook Time*

 **6** SERVINGS *Makes*

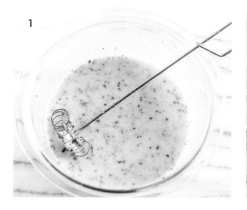

1

2

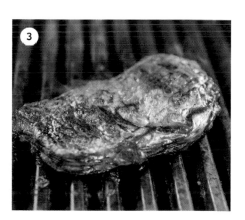

3

# ITALIAN CHOPPED SALAD

I love a salad that eats like a meal.

It's sort of my way of having something healthy but filling it with so many tasty ingredients that I don't feel like I'm missing out. One of my favorites is an Italian Chopped Salad. Basically, it's lettuce mixed with pizza toppings, so you feel like you're getting a treat but all those meats and veggies make it perfect for anyone on a high-protein diet.

# INGREDIENTS

8 cups finely shredded lettuce (iceberg or romaine)

4 Roma tomatoes, diced

2 green bell peppers, diced

½ cup diced salami

½ cup diced pepperoni

½ cup diced ham

1 (14-ounce) can garbanzo beans, rinsed

¼ cup sliced black olives

4 to 6 pepperoncini, sliced

1 cup Monterey Jack cheese, cubed

½ cup pistachios, chopped

## DRESSING:

¼ cup olive oil

¼ cup red wine vinegar

2 tablespoons Dijon mustard

2 garlic cloves, minced

¼ cup grated Parmesan cheese

1 teaspoon salt

1 teaspoon black pepper

# DIRECTIONS

1. *Toss together all of the salad ingredients in a large salad or mixing bowl, tossing with tongs to fully combine and get everything distributed evenly.*

2. *Combine all of the dressing ingredients in a bowl. Cover tightly with lid and* shake vigorously for about 1 minute (or so). Give it a taste and adjust seasonings accordingly.

3. *Toss the salad with as much or as little dressing as you'd like. Serve right away.*

 **15 MIN** *Prep Time*

 **8 SERVINGS** *Makes*

2

# ZESTY MEXICAN SALAD
## *with Chili-Rubbed Salmon*

I did not grow up eating fish. Or, I guess I did if you count Van de Kamps fish sticks. It wasn't until I was an adult that I really began to embrace seafood, and one of my favorites, as in, I eat it at least once a week, is this chili-rubbed salmon. We often make extra so we can take it the next day for work, and it's great warmed up or served cold. The zesty salad is an awesome base for this, but you can truly serve it with anything.

# INGREDIENTS

8 cups chopped romaine

2 cups chopped tomatoes

1½ cups corn

½ cup chopped red onion

1 cup crumbled queso fresco, or feta cheese

1 ripe avocado, cubed

1 (14-ounce) can black beans, rinsed

½ cup chopped cilantro

1 tablespoon Fiesta Blend

1 teaspoon chili powder

4 salmon fillets (1 pound)

## DRESSING:

½ cup olive oil

¼ cup freshly squeezed lime juice

1 tablespoon honey mustard

2 teaspoons Fiesta Blend

1 garlic clove, minced

½ teaspoon salt

# DIRECTIONS

1. *Preheat the oven to 450°F.*

2. *Whisk together all the ingredients for the dressing until it's completely emulsified, and set it aside.*

3. *Place the romaine, tomatoes, corn, red onion, crumbled cheese, avocado, black beans, and cilantro into a large serving bowl.*

4. *Mix together the Fiesta Blend and chili powder in a small bowl. Rub the mixture into the salmon fillets, coating all sides.*

*Place the salmon on a parchment-lined baking sheet, and bake until just barely done in the center. For a 1-inch fillet this takes about 5 to 8 minutes.*

5. *Serve the salmon fillets with the salad and dressing.*

 **25 MIN** *Prep Time*

 **5 MIN** *Cook Time*

 **4 SERVINGS** *Makes*

# LAYERED ANTIPASTO SALAD

Antipasto always reminds me of summertime and wine and noshing for hours at the table in our backyard. This recipe is a great combination of all those flavors we love so much on an alfresco summer night. I highly recommend it for a potluck or as a great option to meal prep and then eat for lunch throughout the week. In that instance, I'd keep the dressing on the side until you're ready to enjoy it to make sure your veggies stay fresh.

# INGREDIENTS

8 cups mixed baby greens

½ cup chopped basil

1 cup chopped salami (4 ounces)

4 to 6 slices of prosciutto (4 ounces), chopped

1 cup cubed fontina cheese

½ cup sliced black olives

6 pepperoncini, thinly sliced

1 cup chopped roasted red bell pepper

1 cup quartered artichoke hearts

2 cups chopped tomatoes

1 cup thinly sliced red onions

1 cup grated Parmesan cheese

## DRESSING:

¼ cup balsamic vinegar

1 teaspoon Zesty Italian seasoning

1 garlic clove, minced

1 teaspoon Dijon mustard

½ teaspoon salt

½ cup olive oil

# DIRECTIONS

1. *Whisk together all the ingredients for the dressing until it's completely emulsified, and set it aside to let the flavors blend.*

2. *Place the mixed greens and basil into a large serving bowl, and toss them together.*

3. *Layer the salami, prosciutto, fontina, olives, pepperoncini, roasted red pepper, artichokes, tomatoes, and onion over the top of the mixed greens.*

4. *Sprinkle with the Parmesan and drizzle with dressing, or serve the salad with the Parmesan and dressing on the side.*

 *Prep Time* — 20 MIN

 *Makes* — 4 SERVINGS

# GRILLED LIME
# CHICKEN FAJITA SALAD

The flavor in this salad is classic fajitas, but what's so great about it is that the protein is totally versatile. You can use chicken breast, shrimp, steak, or even go strictly vegetarian, and it's going to be just as delicious.

# INGREDIENTS

1 tablespoon Fiesta Blend

2 boneless, skinless chicken breasts (1 pound)

1 tablespoon olive oil

1 tablespoon freshly squeezed lime juice

1 red bell pepper, thinly sliced

1 yellow bell pepper, thinly sliced

1 onion, thinly sliced

8 cups chopped romaine

2 cups cherry tomatoes, halved

1 cup crumbled queso fresco, or feta cheese

1 large ripe avocado, thinly sliced

¼ cup chopped cilantro

## DRESSING:

¼ cup freshly squeezed lime juice

2 garlic cloves, minced

2 tablespoons chopped cilantro

2 tablespoons Fiesta Blend

½ teaspoon salt

½ cup olive oil

# DIRECTIONS

1. Whisk together all the ingredients for the dressing until emulsified, and set it aside to let the flavors blend. It will separate as it sits, so whisk it together again right before serving.

2. Preheat a grill over medium heat until it reaches a steady temperature between 350° and 400°F. Rub the Fiesta Blend over the surface of the chicken breasts, and drizzle the lime juice over the top.

3. Grill the chicken for about 8 minutes per side, or until no longer pink in the center. When the chicken is done, set it aside to cool while you assemble the rest of the salad.

4. Heat a medium-size skillet over medium-high heat. When the pan is hot, add the olive oil, red pepper, yellow pepper, and onions to the pan. Sauté until the veggies are just tender, 4 to 5 minutes, and set them aside to cool slightly.

5. Place the romaine, cherry tomatoes, crumbled cheese, avocado, and cilantro in a large serving bowl.

6. Cut the chicken into bite-size pieces, and layer it in the salad bowl with the sautéed peppers and onions.

7. Drizzle with dressing, or serve the salad and dressing separately as desired.

 *Prep Time*

 *Cook Time*

 *Makes*

# LOADED LENTIL SALAD

Lentils get a bad rap. They're super versatile, high in fiber, and they hold up really well. Meaning, while your romaine lettuce is going to get soggy in about thirteen seconds, your lentil salad will still be great three days later. I also love the idea that you can keep these stored in the pantry until you're ready to use them and then mix up the salad with the fresh veggies you have on hand.

# INGREDIENTS

1 cup green lentils, rinsed

2 cups parsnips, peeled and chopped into bite-size pieces

2 cups carrots, peeled and chopped into bite-size pieces

1 red onion, finely diced

1 tablespoon olive oil

½ cup chopped pistachios

½ cup chopped cilantro

6 thinly sliced radishes

## DRESSING:

2 teaspoons Moroccan Seasoning

¼ cup freshly squeezed lemon juice

1 garlic clove, minced

⅓ cup olive oil

2 tablespoons Greek yogurt

½ teaspoon salt

# DIRECTIONS

1. *Preheat the oven to 425°F and line a baking sheet with parchment paper.*

2. *Place the lentils into a medium-size saucepan, and cover with 3 cups of water. Bring the lentils to a boil, boil for 5 minutes, then reduce the heat to low. Cover the pan and simmer until the lentils are tender, about 45 minutes. Stir occasionally, and add extra water if needed. When the lentils are tender, drain and add them to a serving or mixing bowl.*

3. *While the lentils are cooking, whisk together all the ingredients for the dressing, and set it aside to let the flavors blend.*

4. *Place the chopped parsnips, carrots, and onions on a baking sheet, and drizzle with the olive oil. Roast the vegetables until tender and caramelized, 20 minutes.*

5. *Mix the roasted vegetables with the cooked lentils, pistachios, cilantro, and radishes.*

6. *Toss the salad with the dressing, season to taste with salt, and serve immediately.*

**20** MIN *Prep Time*

**45** MIN *Cook Time*

**4** SERVINGS *Makes*

# QUINOA AND KALE SALAD
## *with Chickpeas*

Every Wednesday the entire staff at Chic Media works from home because every single person on staff is a millennial and, apparently, this is SOP if you're under thirty working in media today. What that actually means is that we all go to coffee shops near our homes and work with headphones on. My coffee shop of choice has a delicious chickpea and kale salad, which is the inspiration for this gorgeous dinner. It's a great option for vegetarians, but you could easily add a more hearty protein if you prefer.

# INGREDIENTS

1 cup quinoa, rinsed

1 (15-ounce) can chickpeas, rinsed

2 cups baby kale, finely chopped

3 mandarin oranges, peeled and thinly sliced

2 blood oranges, peeled and thinly sliced

¼ cup chopped dried cranberries

¼ cup toasted pumpkin seeds

## DRESSING:

¼ cup tahini

¼ cup freshly squeezed lemon juice

½ cup freshly squeezed orange juice

1 garlic clove, minced

¼ cup olive oil

½ teaspoon salt

½ teaspoon ground cumin

# DIRECTIONS

1. *Place the quinoa in a medium-size saucepan, and cover with 2 cups water. Bring the quinoa to a boil, then cover the pan and reduce the heat to low. Simmer until the quinoa has absorbed the liquid and is tender. Turn the heat off, and let the quinoa sit another 5 minutes for a fluffier texture. Let the quinoa cool for about 20 minutes, or until warm instead of hot, before mixing it together with the salad ingredients.*

2. *Meanwhile, whisk together all the ingredients for the dressing until completely emulsified, and set it aside.*

3. *When the quinoa has cooked and cooled, mix it together with the chickpeas, kale, sliced oranges, cranberries, and pumpkin seeds.*

4. *Add the dressing, and mix thoroughly to fully combine the salad and dressing.*

5. *Season to taste with salt and serve immediately.*

 **20** MIN *Cook Time*

 **25** MIN *Prep Time*

 **4-6** SERVINGS *Makes*

# FATTOUSH SALAD

Anytime a salad lists bread—or in this case, pita chips—as a signature ingredient, I'm in. This is a classic Mediterranean dish and perfect served alongside hummus and tzatziki and some kind of grilled meat . . . Check out the grilling chapter for pairing ideas.

# INGREDIENTS

1 head romaine, chopped and washed (6 to 8 cups)

2 cups cherry tomatoes, quartered

1 hothouse cucumber, halved lengthwise and thinly sliced

½ cup thinly sliced radishes

1 cup thinly sliced red onion

½ cup chopped parsley

¼ cup chopped mint

## PITA CHIPS:

3 (6-inch) whole-wheat pitas, cut into bite-size pieces (2 cups)

1 teaspoon Moroccan Seasoning

2 tablespoons olive oil

## DRESSING:

¼ cup freshly squeezed lemon juice

1 garlic clove, minced

½ cup olive oil

½ teaspoon salt

1 tablespoon Moroccan Seasoning

# DIRECTIONS

1. *Preheat the oven to 400°F and line a baking sheet with parchment paper.*

2. *Mix together the cut-up pita bread with the Moroccan Seasoning and olive oil until combined. Spread the pita pieces evenly on the baking sheet, and bake until golden brown with crispy edges, about 10 minutes. Set the pita chips aside to cool as you make the salad.*

3. *Whisk together all the ingredients for the dressing until completely emulsified, and set it aside to let the flavors blend. The dressing will separate as it sits, so whisk it together again right before serving.*

4. *For the salad, place the romaine, tomatoes, cucumber, radishes, red onion, parsley, and mint in a large serving bowl.*

5. *Top the salad with the pita chips, and drizzle with dressing, or serve the dressing on the side as desired.*

6. *Serve immediately.*

 **20** MIN *Prep Time*

 **10** MIN *Cook Time*

 **4** SERVINGS *Makes*

# TUNA STUFFED AVOCADOS

Tuna salad is one of the items I usually always have on hand in the fridge. It's high in protein and a great source of omegas, so I typically make some on Sundays and then eat it throughout the week. That makes this dinner the easiest thing on the planet. I just slice open a ripe avocado and add a scoop of salad to the middle. I've also seen people do this with crab and salmon salad as well.

# INGREDIENTS

1 (5-ounce) can tuna fish, packed in water (¾ cup)

¼ cup Greek yogurt

2 teaspoons honey mustard

¼ cup chopped roasted red bell pepper

1 tablespoon chopped basil

½ teaspoon salt

¼ teaspoon black pepper

2 ripe avocados, halved, with pits removed

# DIRECTIONS

1. *Drain the tuna fish, and thoroughly mix it with the yogurt, mustard, red bell pepper, and basil. Season to taste with salt and black pepper.*

2. *Scoop a small amount of avocado from each half to widen the "bowl" area. Chop the extra avocado, and mix it into the tuna salad mixture.*

3. *Fill each avocado half with one quarter of the filling and serve immediately.*

**15** MIN *Prep Time*

**2-4** SERVINGS *Makes*

# SIDES FOR DINNER

Every year for our anniversary, Dave and I go to a restaurant in Beverly Hills called Mastro's Steakhouse. Now, Mastro's, for those of you who've never had the pleasure, is a Los Angeles institution. It's been around since I don't even know when and it requires both making a reservation months beforehand and a dinner jacket. The day of your dinner you'll get a call from someone—he says he's the maître d' but honestly, you guys, I'm pretty sure it's the voice-over actor they hire out to do just this job. This guy sounds like he's confirming your reservation with the royal family; he assures you they *cannot wait* to welcome you into their space. You arrive at dinner in something spiffy . . . . You likely wore the highest heels you own because you've only got to make it from the valet stand to your table. Once inside, a bright young thing will either seat you downstairs (for ordinary plebeians) or escort you up a long and winding staircase to the promised land

Upstairs at Mastro's is the greatest people watching you'll ever do in your whole life. The bar itself stretches the length of the room and is roughly the size of the ships that brought my ancestors here from Ireland. In the middle of the room is a grand piano being manhandled by someone old enough to be your grandpa. Throughout the night you'll hear him play Sinatra and Billie Holiday and then every once in a while you'll ask yourself, wait, is that Hotline Bling?

Everywhere you look are basically the wealthiest people you've ever seen, and if you didn't grow up in that kind of space, then it's impossible to take it all in stride. In the corner is a gorgeous model in her early twenties. The old man across the table *is not her dad*, he's her date. At the table beside you are two men who look like vagabonds . . . . The restaurant waived whatever wardrobe requirements they typically have since they're both Oscar winners.

You'll order a martini the size of a Nissan Sentra and begin to peruse a menu made famous by their cuts of meat and their butter cake. It's all magic, but if you ask me, the greatest thing about Mastro's isn't the martinis or the people-watching or even the piano player, *God bless him* . . . it's the side dishes. This restaurant boasts the greatest menu of side dishes you will ever witness.

Ever.

Buttery lobster mashed potatoes, beer-battered onion rings the size of your face, truffle mac 'n' cheese that *will* make you cry it's so good. In fact, while Dave orders the steak . . . I make a meal out of all the sides and whichever white wine is cheapest on the menu. It's one of my favorite nights of the year. So when I started to plan out the chapters for this book and I asked myself if side dishes could really be considered dinner all on their own, I thought of Mastro's. Side dishes can team up to be a delicious meal for you and your family, or you can serve them alongside an entrée and really go to town. I'd suggest eating these with some jazzy piano music in the background.

# GARLIC-HERB SMASHED POTATOES

Remember Bubba in *Forrest Gump* and how he could name every kind of shrimp dish? That's me with potatoes. You want them fried? Boiled? Twice baked? Mashed? Scalloped? You want them sweet or savory or loaded down with all the fixings? I will gladly join you! Given how much I love and adore this vegetable, you can understand how surprised I was to discover *smashed* potatoes a couple of years ago. I had no idea this was even a thing . . . . How did I miss it for so many years? Thank the good Lord for Pinterest, because this recipe is everything you imagine it could be and more. It makes the perfect side dish or base for adding toppings to make these puppies your entire meal.

# INGREDIENTS

6 small red potatoes (1 pound)

Cooking spray

2 tablespoons salted butter, melted

1 garlic clove, minced

½ teaspoon Zesty Italian seasoning

1 tablespoon finely chopped parsley

¼ cup grated Parmesan cheese

Salt and black pepper

# DIRECTIONS

1. Place the unpeeled potatoes in a large saucepan, cover with water to 2 inches above the potatoes, and bring the pan to a boil. Reduce the heat to medium, and simmer until the potatoes are tender, 20 to 25 minutes depending on the size of the potatoes.

2. Preheat the oven to 450°F, and lightly coat a baking sheet with cooking spray.

3. Drain the potatoes and place them on a baking sheet. Using a potato masher, carefully smash the potatoes until they are flattened, but still holding together in one piece.

4. Mix together the melted butter, garlic, Zesty Italian seasoning, and parsley.

5. Evenly drizzle the garlic butter mixture over each of the six smashed potatoes. Sprinkle each potato with the Parmesan, and season with salt and black pepper.

6. Bake the smashed potatoes until golden brown with crispy edges, 10 to 12 minutes.

7. Serve immediately.

 **15** MIN *Prep Time*

 **35** MIN *Cook Time*

**4** SERVINGS *Makes*

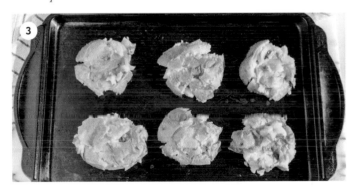

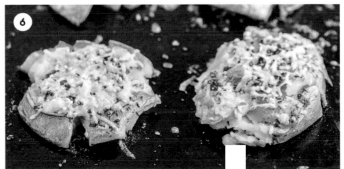

# STREET CORN SALAD

Have you ever had street corn? Before you answer, allow me to clarify. I'm not talking about some hipster creation off a truck at your local farmer's market. I'm describing corn served out of a contraband shopping cart by someone the neighborhood calls Abuelita. I'm talking hot corn pulled from an ice chest then slathered with mayonnaise from a jar that's never once been refrigerated, then dropped into a pile of cheese stored in a Rubbermaid container. If you've never had it this way, if you didn't grow up in a predominantly Hispanic neighborhood like I did . . . then sister, you are missing out! This side dish is my attempt to bring a little bit of those vibrant flavors to your kitchen table. It's an incredible dish to serve alongside something from the grill.

# INGREDIENTS

2 teaspoons olive oil

3 cups frozen corn, thawed and drained

4 cups mixed baby greens

1 (15-ounce) can black beans, rinsed

½ cup crumbled cotija cheese, or feta cheese

¼ cup chopped cilantro

1 cup diced red onion

1 ripe avocado, cubed

## DRESSING:

½ cup crème fraîche, or sour cream

¼ cup freshly squeezed lime juice

1 garlic clove, minced

1 teaspoon Fiesta Blend

Salt to taste

# DIRECTIONS

1. Preheat a large skillet over medium-high heat. When the pan is hot, add 1 teaspoon of the olive oil, and half of the corn kernels. Toast the corn kernels until browned, 4 to 6 minutes, and repeat the process with the remaining corn and olive oil. Set the toasted corn aside while you assemble the salad.

2. Mix together all the ingredients for the dressing, and set it aside to let the flavors blend.

3. Place the mixed greens into a serving bowl or onto a platter.

4. Mix together the toasted corn, black beans, crumbled cheese, cilantro, red onion, and avocado. Stir in the dressing, and mix to combine. Season the corn mixture with salt to taste.

5. Spoon the corn mixture over the mixed greens, and serve immediately.

 **20** MIN *Prep Time*

 **10** MIN *Cook Time*

 **4** SERVINGS *Makes*

3

4

5

# BALSAMIC ROASTED CARROTS

### *with Ricotta*

Have you ever noticed how certain kinds of food become trendy?

For a while Brussels sprouts were everywhere. Then kale became the new "it" veggie. Because I'm a foodie nerd, I always try and figure out what's going to trend next, and one night while having dinner in New York I realized I knew the answer: roasted carrots! Roasted carrots were the next big thing, and for a while, they, too, had their moment in restaurant stardom, which is how this recipe came to be. A little balsamic here, a little cheese there, and voilà, we made our version of this trendy side.

# INGREDIENTS

2 pounds baby carrots, peeled and trimmed

2 tablespoons balsamic vinegar

1 tablespoon olive oil

½ teaspoon salt

¼ teaspoon black pepper

½ cup panko bread crumbs

¼ cup chopped fresh parsley

## RICOTTA:

1 cup ricotta cheese

2 tablespoons lemon juice

1 garlic clove, minced

pinch of salt

pinch of black pepper

# DIRECTIONS

1. Preheat oven to 375°F.

2. Place the carrots on a baking sheet and toss around with the balsamic vinegar, olive oil, salt, and black pepper. Shake the pan to get the carrots in a single layer. Roast until charred and crispy, about 15 to 20 minutes. About 5 minutes before the carrots are done, remove from the oven and top with the bread crumbs and parsley. Return to oven for remaining 5 minutes.

3. Meanwhile, in a small bowl, stir the ricotta, lemon juice, garlic, salt, and black pepper until evenly combined.

4. Serve the carrots warm with the ricotta on top or on the side for dipping.

 **10** MIN *Prep Time*

 **20** MIN *Cook Time*

 **4** SERVINGS *Makes*

# CRISPY BRUSSELS SPROUTS

I had these Brussels sprouts for the first time at our local sushi joint, if you can believe it. Dave and I went there for our weekly date night, and the waiter talked about this dish with the reverence reserved for heroes and legends. As a great rule for life in general, if your server loves a particular item on the menu to distraction, it's likely the best order you can make. So even though I wasn't super familiar with Brussels sprouts, I ordered it. The next day I set about figuring out how to make them myself. This masterpiece is the result of that endeavor.

# INGREDIENTS

1 pound Brussels sprouts

½ cup almonds, slivered

½ cup sliced scallions

1 tablespoon olive oil

1 teaspoon salt

1 teaspoon black pepper

½ cup balsamic vinegar

2 tablespoons low-sodium soy sauce

1 tablespoon honey

# DIRECTIONS

1. *Preheat oven to 425°F. Line a baking sheet with foil, and set aside.*

2. *Use a paring knife to cut the Brussels sprouts in half. Then, separate the leaves as best you can. Toss the leaves, almonds, scallions, oil, salt, and black pepper in a large bowl. Spread them out into one even layer onto the prepared baking sheet. Roast for about 10 to 15 minutes, or until crispy and slightly charred.*

3. *In the meantime, make the sauce. In a small pot, combine the balsamic vinegar, soy sauce, and honey. Cook over low heat until it is reduced by half and is syrupy. Pour over the Brussels sprouts and toss to fully coat. Enjoy right away!*

 **10** MIN *Prep Time*

 **15** MIN *Cook Time*

 **6** SERVINGS *Makes*

# CILANTRO-LIME RICE

This is straight-up a play on my obsession with my favorite Mexican grill. As a family we attend our local Chipotle almost every Sunday after church, and their rice is just so dang good I had to try it out in my own kitchen. It's a great way to reinvent what could easily become a boring side dish, adding tons of flavor and very little additional calories.

## INGREDIENTS

1 tablespoon olive oil

1 cup finely diced onion

2 garlic cloves, minced

1 teaspoon ground cumin

1½ cups long-grain brown rice

3 cups water

1 teaspoon salt

¼ teaspoon black pepper

¼ cup chopped cilantro

¼ cup freshly squeezed lime juice

## DIRECTIONS

1. Place a medium-size saucepan over medium-high heat. Add the olive oil, onion, and garlic to the pan. Sauté until the onion is softened and translucent, about 5 minutes.

2. Add the cumin and rice to the pan, and cook, stirring until the rice is coated, 1 minute.

3. Add the water, salt, and black pepper to the pan. Bring the rice to a boil, then cover and reduce the heat to low. Simmer until the rice is tender and the liquid has been absorbed, 45 to 50 minutes.

4. When the rice is done, remove it from the heat, and stir in the cilantro and lime juice.

5. Serve immediately.

 *Prep Time* — **10 MIN**

 *Cook Time* — **1 HOUR**

 *Makes* — **4–6 SERVINGS**

# JALAPEÑO MASHED POTATOES

When we were on vacation a few years ago, we went to dinner and the side dish they served was Jalapeño Mashed Potatoes. They were the bomb. Actually, they were the bomb dot com. They were so good, I have to go back to the nineties for a description of them. Guys, you have to add this to your side dish arsenal. They've got just the right kick of heat and garlic and pesto to make your taste buds sing.

## INGREDIENTS

2 pounds russet potatoes, peeled and cubed

2 cups loose fresh basil leaves

2 garlic cloves, peeled

1 to 2 jalapeños, seeded and chopped

¼ cup grated Parmesan cheese

¼ cup pine nuts

2 teaspoons salt

2 teaspoons black pepper

⅓ to ½ cup olive oil

4 tablespoons unsalted butter

½ cup whole milk or buttermilk

## DIRECTIONS

1. *Place the potatoes in a large pot. Cover with cold water and bring to a boil. Cook until fork tender, about 15 to 20 minutes. Drain and return to pot or transfer to a bowl.*

2. *In a food processor or blender, combine the basil, jalapeño, garlic, Parmesan cheese, pine nuts, 1 teaspoon of the salt, and 1 teaspoon of the black pepper. Pulse until chopped. While the machine* is running, slowly stream in the olive oil until a pourable sauce forms. You might need less or more olive oil.

3. *Mash the potatoes with the butter and milk until smooth. Season with the remaining 1 teaspoon salt and 1 teaspoon black pepper. Stir in the pesto until well combined. Serve warm as a side dish.*

 **20** MIN *Prep Time*

 **20** MIN *Cook Time*

 **8** SERVINGS *Makes*

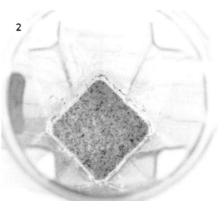

# ROASTED RANCH CAULIFLOWER

I did not grow up eating cauliflower, and until a few years ago I wouldn't even consider it as part of my lineup. But then I tried to cut out meat from my diet, and I had to look for filling alternatives to add to dishes like stir-fry. Everywhere I looked, this veggie was in play as a great substitute and so I gave it a whirl. I love how versatile it is. I've made buffalo cauliflower and mashed cauliflower and, in this case, roasted it with some simple seasoning as an easy and filling side dish.

# INGREDIENTS

1 head cauliflower (8 cups), trimmed and cut into florets

1 tablespoon Southwestern Ranch seasoning

2 tablespoons olive oil

½ cup thinly sliced scallions

½ teaspoon salt

# DIRECTIONS

1. Preheat the oven to 350°F.

2. Toss together the cauliflower florets, Southwestern Ranch seasoning, olive oil, scallions, and salt.

3. Spread the florets evenly on a baking sheet, and roast until tender, about 15 minutes.

4. Serve immediately.

 **10** MIN *Prep Time*

 **15** MIN *Cook Time*

**4** SERVINGS *Makes*

# CRISPY SWEET POTATO BAKE

Dave Hollis and I have been having a disagreement since the day we met. He likes things crunchy and I like things soft. Cookies? He wants them crispy like a chip. I want them warm and chewy. Bread? He wants it toasted to a sharp crunch. Me? I want it pillowy and covered with butter. When it comes to sweet potatoes, I can eat them baked or mashed . . . The softness doesn't bother me, but he still needs a crispy edge to make it palatable. This crispy sweet potato bake is our middle ground. It's crispy on top and moist on bottom, making it the perfect side dish for any time of year.

# INGREDIENTS

2 sweet potatoes (2 pounds)

2 tablespoons olive oil

1 tablespoon chopped fresh rosemary

1 garlic clove, minced

1 teaspoon salt

½ teaspoon black pepper

# DIRECTIONS

**1.** Preheat the oven to 375°F.

**2.** Cut both ends off the sweet potatoes and peel them. Thinly slice both sweet potatoes into ¼-inch thick slices.

**3.** Layer the potato slices in an 8- or 9-inch cast-iron skillet in concentric circles.

**4.** Mix together the olive oil, rosemary, garlic, salt, and black pepper in a small bowl.

**5.** Brush the olive oil mixture evenly over the top of the potato slices, cover the pan tightly with foil, and bake for 45 minutes or until just tender.

**6.** When the sweet potatoes are just tender, remove the foil, and increase the heat to 475°F. Bake until the edges are browned and crispy, 10 to 15 minutes.

**7.** Serve immediately.

**20** MIN — Prep Time

**1** HOUR — Cook Time

**4** SERVINGS — Makes

# GRILLED ZUCCHINI SPEARS

These grilled zucchini are my second-favorite spears . . . . Britney is obviously my first. Can you blame me? I stood transfixed like every other fifteen-year-old watching TRL when the "Baby One More Time" video came out. Later, when she wore entirely red pleather for "Oops! . . . I Did It Again," I was right there with her. Me and Brit Brit go way back. Me and zucchini, well, that's a more recent friendship, but no less relevant.

# INGREDIENTS

2 to 4 zucchini (2 pounds)    1 tablespoon olive oil    ½ teaspoon salt    1 lemon, cut into wedges

1 garlic clove, minced    1 teaspoon Zesty Italian seasoning

# DIRECTIONS

1. *Preheat a grill over high heat until it reaches 450°F.*

2. *Meanwhile, cut both ends off the zucchini, and cut them lengthwise into spears, about 1 inch thick.*

3. *Mix together the garlic, olive oil, Zesty Italian seasoning, and salt in a small bowl.*

4. *Toss the zucchini spears with the olive oil mixture.*

5. *When the grill has reached 450°F, lay the zucchini spears evenly over the surface of the grill. Immediately lower the heat to medium, maintaining a temperature of 350° to 400°F.*

6. *Grill the zucchini spears for 5 minutes per side, or until tender, and serve immediately with lemon wedges.*

**10** MIN *Prep Time*

**10** MIN *Cook Time*

**4** SERVINGS *Makes*

# MY FAVORITE DINNERS

At church on Sunday we were talking about the definition of "shalom." The idea of a peace that passes understanding is something that many religions and denominations can identify with. The question was, what are the things in your life that bring you shalom . . . what brings you true peace? What makes you feel centered?

For me, one of the most peaceful experiences in my life is getting to cook my favorite food for my favorite people. Not just the rushed weeknight meal, but the recipes that I can take a little extra time with because it's a weekend. I pour a glass of wine, put on some country music or some Fleetwood Mac, and put love into every bite.

As I was making a list of recipes for this book, there were a handful of those dishes that are my ultimate favorites and therefore they needed their own special category. For instance . . . the fried chicken I make for Sunday supper didn't fit neatly in another chapter. Or the cauliflower stir-fry that we have once a week for dinner now that my diet is mostly meat-free . . . where would that go? So rather than leave them out, I just decided to have a chapter of my favorites. These are the entrées I reach for most often, or the ones that my husband or kids beg for time after time. These are the greatest of all my greatest, and I hope they bring you a similar sense of peace that they bring me.

# BUTTERMILK FRIED CHICKEN

I almost included this recipe in my first cookbook, but I worried that it was too time-consuming for most people to attempt. But it's book two, and I think we're all in a place where we can commit a little time to some extra delicious flavor. I have been perfecting this buttermilk marinade for years, as well as testing temperature options and what to fry in. The end result is one of the things I'm most proud of in this world. I can't wait to hear what you think!

# INGREDIENTS

1 tablespoon cayenne

1 tablespoon dried thyme

1 tablespoon dried tarragon

1 quart buttermilk

1 cup butter-flavored Crisco

2 cups all-purpose flour

½ white onion, cut into rings or strips

1 whole fryer chicken cut into pieces, or 4 pounds chicken tenders

Salt, black pepper, and more cayenne for seasoning

# DIRECTIONS

1. In a large bowl, mix together the cayenne, thyme, tarragon, buttermilk, and onions until combined. Remove the chicken from packaging, thoroughly rinse with water, and pat dry with paper towels. Add the chicken to the buttermilk mixture, and make sure the chicken is coated and submerged in the buttermilk. Then cover the bowl with foil or plastic wrap and refrigerate 8 hours or overnight.

2. When you're ready to cook the chicken, add 1 cup of Crisco to a 9-inch cast-iron skillet. Turn the heat to medium, and let the Crisco melt while you prepare the chicken.

3. In a shallow dish, add the flour and season heavily with salt, black pepper, and a dash of cayenne. Before you add any chicken to the pan, taste a bit of the flour mixture. If it tastes bland, add more seasonings.

4. Once you have your flour seasoned, take one piece of chicken out of the marinade, and allow the excess to drip off before dredging both sides in the flour mixture.

5. Place the dredged chicken in the skillet, taking care not to splash the oil. Continue dredging pieces of chicken until your pan is full.

6. For the chicken tenders, cook for at least 10 minutes or until chicken is no longer pink in the center.

7. For whole fryer pieces, cook low and slow, about 20 minutes per pan, turning the chicken several times throughout the cooking time until the chicken is no longer pink in the center.

8. Repeat the dredging and frying process with the remaining pieces of chicken. To keep the fried pieces of chicken warm while you fry the remaining pieces, line a baking sheet with paper towels, and top with a wire rack. Add the fried chicken to the baking sheet and keep it warm in an oven preheated to 200°F.

 **8** HOURS *Prep Time*

 **30-45** MIN *Cook Time*

 **4-6** SERVINGS *Makes*

# SPINACH CHICKEN BAKE

As a sort of joke, when Ford was a baby I tried to figure out if there was a recipe I could make one-handed. The idea was that there must be a dinner I could create with a baby on my hip—there's even an old video somewhere on YouTube of me doing it with this exact dish. It's an easy-peasy dinner and the perfect option for low-carb diets because it's only veggies, chicken, and cheese. Baby not included.

# INGREDIENTS

1 tablespoon olive oil

1 (6-ounce) bag baby spinach

1 pound sliced mushrooms

1 teaspoon salt

1 teaspoon black pepper

1 (14-ounce) can diced tomatoes

6 boneless, skinless chicken breasts (about 3 pounds)

12 slices provolone cheese

## OPTIONAL:

1 tablespoon chopped fresh parsley for color

# DIRECTIONS

1. *Set a large skillet over medium-high heat. Add the olive oil and sauté the spinach and mushrooms until wilted, about 5 minutes. Season with a bit of salt and black pepper. Stir in the tomatoes and cook until reduced by half, about 10 minutes.*

2. *Grease a 9- by 13-inch baking dish and set the chicken in a single layer. Season with salt and black pepper. Lay 2 slices of cheese on top of each chicken breast, and pour the sauce and veggies over the chicken.*

3. *Bake for about 25 to 30 minutes at 375°F. Remove from oven, sprinkle with parsley, and serve immediately.*

 **15** MIN — *Prep Time*

 **30** MIN — *Cook Time*

 **6** SERVINGS — *Makes*

# CAULIFLOWER STIR-FRY

This recipe is a newer addition to my weekly lineup. When I decided to give up eating meat, I needed new options I could cook for the whole family that would serve all of our dietary needs. This stir-fry works for all of us because I can add in chicken breast for Dave and the boys while I just eat the cauliflower and other veggies. Anytime I can create one dish that effectively feeds the whole family, I feel like I'm winning.

## INGREDIENTS

2 tablespoons olive oil

1 large head cauliflower, cut into 1- to 2-inch florets

1 large red bell pepper, diced

1 small head broccoli, cut into florets

2 carrots, peeled and thinly sliced (2 cups)

1 tablespoon minced fresh ginger

1 cup sliced scallions (reserve half for garnishing)

1 clove garlic, minced

½ cup sweet chili sauce

2 tablespoons soy sauce

½ cup roughly chopped cilantro

½ cup roasted peanuts

1 lime, cut into wedges

3 cups of cooked rice

## DIRECTIONS

1. *Heat a large (12- to 15-inch) skillet over medium-high heat. When the pan is hot but not smoking, add the olive oil, cauliflower, red bell pepper, and carrots. Sauté, stirring as the veggies begin to brown for 2 to 3 minutes. Then partially cover the pan with a lid and cook, stirring as needed for another 2 to 3 minutes, or until the cauliflower is almost tender.*

2. *Remove the lid from the skillet, and add the broccoli, half the scallions (reserving the rest for garnishing), ginger, and garlic. Cook, stirring as the vegetables continue to brown until they're crisp-tender, about 5 minutes.*

3. *Add the sweet chili sauce and soy sauce to the pan and stir to combine. Remove the pan from the heat and garnish with the remaining scallions, cilantro, and peanuts.*

4. *Serve the stir-fry with the lime wedges on the side for squeezing over the top.*

 **20** MIN *Prep Time*

 **10–15** MIN *Cook Time*

 **4** SERVINGS *Makes*

# CRAB CAKES

I was going to say that crab cakes are extra fancy . . . and then I wondered if maybe they're only fancy to me because I didn't grow up eating them. The very fact that they're a "cake" instead of straight seafood probably means that actual fancy people aren't impressed by them. Oh well, I think they're cool and delicious, and since I eat so much seafood, now they've become a favorite to make at home.

# INGREDIENTS

1 pound lump crab meat
(I used Dungeness)

1 tablespoon freshly squeezed
lemon juice

2 tablespoons snipped fresh chives

¼ cup red bell pepper, finely diced

1 tablespoon snipped fresh dill

1 egg, beaten

3 tablespoons Greek yogurt

⅔ cup whole-wheat bread crumbs
(or gluten-free)

½ teaspoon salt

½ teaspoon black pepper

Cooking oil (I used avocado oil)

1 lemon, cut into wedges for serving

# DIRECTIONS

1. Place all the ingredients except the cooking oil and lemon wedges into a medium-size mixing bowl. Mix the ingredients together, taking care not to break up the lumps of crab meat too much.

2. Preheat a large (12-inch) skillet over medium heat, and form the crab mixture into 8 to 10 cakes/patties, 3 inches in diameter by 1 inch thick.

3. Add 2 tablespoons of cooking oil to the preheated pan along with 3 of the formed crab cakes. Cook until golden brown before flipping the crab cakes, about 1 to 2 minutes per side.

4. Continue the cooking process, adding small amounts of cooking oil as needed, until all the crab cakes are done. Keep the cooked crab cakes in a warm oven to keep them hot as you finish cooking the rest.

5. Serve the crab cakes with the lemon wedges.

 Prep Time

 Cook Time

 Makes

# SHRIMP FRIED RICE

Oh my gosh you guys, shrimp fried rice is my favorite! Seriously, what's not to love here? It's got all the great flavor of my takeout but I don't feel like a terrible human feeding it to my kids because I know exactly what went into every step. Also, it's super easy to substitute for chicken or beef if you want to go all out. Extra credit if you add some bacon in at the veggie sautéing stage.

# INGREDIENTS

1 tablespoon olive oil

1 pound shrimp, peeled and deveined

1 teaspoon salt

1 teaspoon black pepper

½ teaspoon chili flakes

¼ cup sliced scallions

2 garlic cloves

4 celery stalks, diced

2 medium carrots, diced

1 teaspoon fresh grated ginger

4 large eggs, lightly beaten

2 cups brown rice (cold)

2 teaspoons soy sauce

½ teaspoon sesame oil

2 cups frozen peas, thawed

# DIRECTIONS

1. *Heat a large skillet over medium-high heat with a tablespoon olive oil. Once hot, add the shrimp and arrange on a single layer. Season with ½ teaspoon salt, ½ teaspoon black pepper, and chili flakes. Cook until pink, stirring to evenly cook. Transfer to a plate and set aside.*

2. *Stir in half of the scallions to the hot skillet, along with the garlic. Cook for a few seconds. Add the celery, carrots and ginger and cook until soft and tender, about 5 to 7 minutes. Make sure to stir often so that it doesn't burn. Push the veggies to one side of the skillet. Add the beaten eggs to the empty side and allow to cook for a minute without touching. Scramble everything together and cook until the eggs are done, about 2 more minutes.*

3. *Stir in the brown rice, soy sauce, sesame oil, remaining ½ teaspoon salt, ½ teaspoon black pepper, peas and shrimp. Lower the flame to low and allow to heat through. Serve and garnish with remaining scallions. Enjoy!*

**15** MIN — *Prep Time*

**25** MIN — *Cook Time*

**6** SERVINGS — *Makes*

# BRAISED CHICKEN LEGS

If you're looking for delicious, heart-warming, and comforting meals without too much work, these oven-braised drumsticks with veggies are the answer. I focused in on drumsticks because it's the part of the chicken my kids like best then I just load up on all the oven-roasted veggies.

# INGREDIENTS

3 tablespoons olive oil

2 pounds chicken legs, cleaned and dried

1 teaspoon salt

1 teaspoon black pepper

1 teaspoon garlic powder

1 teaspoon paprika

½ teaspoon dried oregano

½ teaspoon cumin

½ teaspoon chili flakes

1 tablespoon Worcestershire sauce

2 cups dry white wine (such as Chardonnay)

1 tablespoon whole grain mustard

2 sprigs fresh rosemary

3 garlic cloves, peeled

1 pound small red potatoes, quartered

4 medium carrots, diced

4 celery stalks, diced

1 red onion, diced

1 red bell pepper, diced

1 lemon, thinly sliced

parsley for garnish

# DIRECTIONS

1. Preheat oven to 450 degrees F.

2. Heat a large heavy-duty dutch oven over medium heat with 2 tablespoons olive oil. In a large bowl, toss together the chicken with all of the seasonings and Worcestershire sauce. Sear the chicken, in batches, for about 2 to 3 minutes per side. We're not looking to cook it all the way through, just browning it. Transfer to a plate or platter and continue browning the rest.

3. Add the wine and mustard to the hot skillet and allow to cook down for about 3 minutes along with the rosemary and garlic. Remove from heat and toss in the vegetables and lemon slices. Arrange the chicken on top of the veggies.

4. Place the pot in the oven and cook for about 50 minutes to 1 hour or until the veggies are tender and the chicken is cooked through and crispy. Remove from oven and allow to cool slightly before serving. Serve chicken with veggies. Garnish with parsley.

**10 MIN** *Prep Time*

**50 MIN** *Cook Time*

**4 SERVINGS** *Makes*

# TURKEY
# LETTUCE WRAPS

This is such a simple dish and one I gravitate to when ground turkey is on special at the grocery store. If you don't eat meat, you can make it with all the ingredients minus the meat and the flavors are still just as yummy.

# INGREDIENTS

1 tablespoon olive oil

2 pounds ground turkey

1 red onion, diced

3 garlic cloves, minced

½ cup sliced scallions

2 medium carrots, diced

2 large celery stalks, diced

1 orange or yellow bell pepper, diced

1 cup shredded savoy cabbage

¼ cup hoisin sauce

2 tablespoons soy sauce

1 to 2 teaspoons sriracha

1 teaspoon salt

1 teaspoon black pepper

1 large iceberg lettuce head, leaves carefully removed

# DIRECTIONS

1. *Heat a large skillet over medium-high heat with 1 tablespoon oil. Add the ground turkey and cook, breaking it down with a wooden spoon, until browned and crispy. Stir in the red onion, garlic, and half of the scallions. Toss and cook for about 3 minutes to soften.*

2. *Add the remaining veggies and cook for another 5 minutes, until tender. Mix in the hoisin, soy sauce, sriracha, salt, and black pepper. Cook for 1 to 2 minutes to thicken the sauce. Serve in lettuce leaves with the remaining scallions as garnish.*

 **10** MIN *Prep Time*

 **20** MIN *Cook Time*

 **4** SERVINGS *Makes*

# AVOCADO TUNA MELT

My mama used to make us tuna melts on English muffins with a slice of American cheese on top. I like to think I've elevated the recipes a bit for my own kids but let's be honest, it's still basically a fancy grilled cheese! Adding in the avocado and the really good bread just elevates it to hipster status.

# INGREDIENTS

1 large tuna can (in water), drained

2 tablespoons red onion, diced

2 tablespoons sliced scallions

1 tablespoon parsley

1 lemon, juiced

3 tablespoons olive oil

1 teaspoon grainy mustard (or Dijon) (optional)

½ teaspoon salt

½ teaspoon black pepper

4 slices bread

2 small tomatoes, sliced

2 avocados

4 slices Swiss cheese

# DIRECTIONS

1. *Preheat broiler.*

2. *In a large bowl, combine the tuna, red onion, scallions, parsley, lemon juice, olive oil, mustard (if using), salt and black pepper. Mix to evenly combine.*

3. *Toast the bread and arrange on a baking sheet. Top each bread with 2 slices of tomato, and a couple slices of avocado.*

*Divide the tuna among each sandwich, piling it on top of the tomato and avocado.*

4. *Lay a slice of cheese on top of the tuna and place under the broiler for a few seconds, just until melted. Serve right away and enjoy!*

 **20** MIN *Prep Time*

 **2** MIN *Cook Time*

**4** SERVINGS *Makes*

# SIMPLE BAKED CHICKEN

I feel like I don't hear enough people talking about how to utilize what's on sale at the grocery store. Growing up, the protein we ate was based entirely on the butcher's special that week, and I still shop similarly. A Simple Baked Chicken is not only a great way to make the "picnic special" into dinner, it's also a guaranteed win with my kids. I recommend buying a bunch of what's on sale and freezing the leftover portions for later.

# INGREDIENTS

4 boneless, skinless chicken breasts (about two pounds)

2 tablespoons Fiesta Blend

1 teaspoon ground cumin

1 teaspoon garlic powder

½ teaspoon salt

1 tablespoon olive oil

3 tablespoons freshly squeezed lime juice, from 1 lime

1 tablespoon honey

1 tablespoon chopped fresh cilantro

1 lime cut into slices

# DIRECTIONS

1. Preheat the oven to 375°F, and place the chicken breasts in a ceramic baking dish.

2. In a small bowl, mix together the Fiesta Blend, cumin, garlic powder, salt, olive oil, lime juice, and honey together until combined. Briefly warming up the honey helps it mix in easier.

3. Pour the spice mixture over the chicken and turn the chicken to coat it evenly in the spice mixture.

4. Place the chicken in the oven and bake until no longer pink in the center, about 25 to 30 minutes.

5. Sprinkle the cilantro over the finished chicken and serve immediately with the lime wedges for squeezing over the top.

 **10** MIN *Prep Time*

 **30** MIN *Cook Time*

 **4** SERVINGS *Makes*

# SLOW COOKER BARBACOA

It took a few tries but I think I finally nailed this slow cooker chipotle barbacoa recipe. For those of you who've never had barbacoa, it's a flavorful Latin pot roast. I dig it because it's got so much flavor in the tang of the vinegar and the heat from the chipotle. I suggest eating it in a bowl with cilantro-lime rice, beans, eight different salsas, etc., but this is also perfection in a taco or a burrito.

# INGREDIENTS

4 teaspoons salt

3 teaspoons black pepper

2 tablespoons olive oil

4- to 6-pound boneless chuck roast

⅓ cup apple cider vinegar

4 garlic cloves, minced

4 teaspoons cumin

2 teaspoons dried oregano

½ teaspoon ground cloves

¾ cup chicken broth

3 tablespoons fresh lime juice

3 to 4 chipotle peppers in adobo sauce

3 bay leaves

1 yellow onion, diced

# DIRECTIONS

1. *Season both sides of the roast with 2 teaspoons of the salt and 2 teaspoons of the black pepper. Set a large pot over medium-high heat with the olive oil. Once hot, add the roast and brown on both sides, about 4 to 5 minutes on each side. Transfer to a slow cooker.*

2. *In a small bowl, whisk together the apple cider vinegar, garlic, remaining salt, remaining black pepper, cumin,* oregano, cloves, chicken broth, lime juice, and chipotle peppers in adobo sauce. Pour over the beef and add the bay leaves and onion. Cook on low for 8 to 10 hours or on high for 4 to 6 hours. It should be tender and falling apart. Remove whole bay leaves. Take two forks and shred. Serve on tacos or burritos or in a bowl!*

**15** MIN — *Prep Time*

**8** HOURS — *Cook Time*

**12** SERVINGS — *Makes*

# BACON-WRAPPED CHICKEN TENDERS

This recipe is a winner. It's a winner with my kids, my husband, and fans of the site, who tell us they use this go-to dish for dinner at least once a week. You can definitely make it in a frying pan—if you're trying to gain weight for a movie role, let's say—but I attempt to make it a bit healthier by baking it.

## INGREDIENTS

12 chicken tenders (about 2 pounds)

1 teaspoon salt

1 teaspoon black pepper

1 teaspoon paprika

1 teaspoon onion powder

1 teaspoon dried oregano

12 slices bacon (about 1 pound)

24 toothpicks

## DIRECTIONS

1. *Preheat oven to 450°F. Line a baking sheet with foil and set a wire cooling rack on top. Set aside.*

2. *In a large bowl, toss together the chicken tenders with the seasonings until well combined. Wrap a piece of bacon tightly around each chicken tender, skewering a toothpick on both ends to secure. Place the chicken on the prepared pan and continue wrapping the rest.*

3. *Bake the chicken until cooked through and browned, about 15 to 20 minutes. Remove from the oven, and set the broiler to high. Carefully remove the toothpicks from the chicken and place under the broiler until crispy on top, about 5 minutes. Serve immediately or let cool and store in an airtight container in the fridge for up to a week.*

**10** MIN  *Prep Time*

**25** MIN  *Cook Time*

**4** SERVINGS  *Makes*

# SPAGHETTI CARBONARA

This is, in reality, one of the more simple pasta dishes you can make . . . but no matter how many times I tell our guests that, they still act astounded when it shows up on the table. Carbonara just sounds fancy, which makes us seem like far more advanced chefs than we actually are.

# INGREDIENTS

½ pound dried spaghetti

4 strips thick-cut bacon (4 ounces), cut into small cubes

3 garlic cloves, thinly sliced (horizontally)

¾ cup finely diced onion

2 large eggs

1 heaping cup shredded Parmesan cheese, plus extra for garnish

1 teaspoon black pepper

2 tablespoons chopped fresh parsley

## SERVE WITH:

Freshly grated Parmesan cheese

Freshly ground black pepper

# DIRECTIONS

1. Cook the spaghetti in a large pot of boiling salted water. Cook to al dente according to pasta package directions. Before draining cooked pasta, reserve about ½ cup cooking water.

2. In a large (10- to 12-inch) skillet, sauté the bacon over medium-high heat. As the bacon cooks, fat will render. You will use that fat to cook and flavor the remaining ingredients.

3. Once the bacon is two thirds done cooking, add the garlic. Stir to combine. Cook for about 30 seconds, and add the onions. Cook until the onions are soft and translucent, and the bacon is browned and crisp.

4. While the bacon mixture is cooking, in a small bowl whisk together the eggs until homogenous. Add the Parmesan cheese and black pepper and stir to combine. Set aside.

5. Add the drained pasta to the skillet. Remove from heat. Pour the cheese-egg mixture over pasta. Work quickly and use kitchen tongs to toss and distribute ingredients together. The heat from the pasta and bacon mixture is enough to cook the eggs. As the cheese melts, continue to toss pasta with tongs to evenly coat noodles with sauce. If pasta looks dry, add 1 tablespoon reserved cooking water and toss. Continue to add small amounts of reserved cooking water only if needed.

6. Add half of the parsley and toss to combine. Garnish with the remaining parsley, grated Parmesan, and black pepper.

7. Serve immediately.

 **10** MIN *Prep Time*

 **20-30** MIN *Cook Time*

 **2** SERVINGS *Makes*

# ACKNOWLEDGMENTS

The biggest, most giant thank-you ever to my incomparable team at Chic Media. Twice now we've built a cookbook from the ground up and while I didn't believe it was possible, this one is even better than the first! Thanks for rallying behind the little details and posing in a hundred thousand faux dinner party photo shoots in exchange for tacos and La Croix.

Thank you to my literary agent, Kevan Lyon, who continues to be my champion, mentor, and guidance counselor.

My appreciation to the whole team at St. Martin's, for taking on another project with me and for all of the hard work to see it through to fruition.

Kari Peters did the lion's share of heavy lifting in this book, with oodles and oodles of gorgeous food photography and recipe production. Kari, you have absolutely exceeded every expectation I had. Thanks, girl!

Thanks too to Corey McClelland, whose design of this book elevated something awesome into another stratosphere entirely.

As always, I am eternally grateful for the outstanding cooks in my family tree who taught me how to make my way around the kitchen. Mama and Daddy. Mema, Grandma Neeley, Aunt Linda, Uncle Joe, my big sisters Melody and Christina, and the countless others who encouraged me to add a bit of this and a dash of that from the time I was old enough to stand beside them at the counter.

And lastly, thank you, thank you, thank you to my best friend/husband/baby daddy, Dave, and the four beautiful babies we get to call our own. It is the greatest blessing in my life to share a table with you all every day.

# INDEX

.